116

A SCRUPULOUS MEANNESS

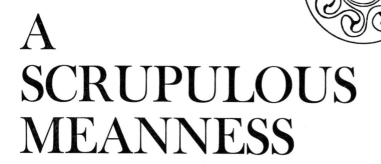

A SCRUPULOUS MEANNESS

A Study of Joyce's Early Work

EDWARD BRANDABUR

University of Illinois Press
URBANA, CHICAGO, & LONDON

His true Penelope was Flaubert,
He fished by obstinate isles.

EZRA POUND
"Hugh Selwyn Mauberley"

for Agnes

PREFACE

THE LIST of those to whom I owe much that is worthwhile in this study is long and distinguished. First of all for the understanding of psychoanalytic theory which I have drawn upon throughout, I am chiefly indebted to Dr. Charleen Schwartz Gallagher of Cincinnati. Her book, *Neurotic Anxiety* (New York, 1954) was a pioneer integration of psychoanalytical insight and moral analysis. Also, she has graciously allowed me to study unpublished material in which she is developing her unique and original work in the causes and therapy of neurosis. I am especially thankful for her suggestion several years ago that I attempt to integrate psychoanalytic insight with the special perceptions of literary criticism: that I avoid the myopia which so often proves a hazard in interdisciplinary studies. My further indebtedness to Northrop Frye and Wilhelm Stekel will, I think, become apparent.

Professor George Ford of the University of Rochester deserves my appreciation far more than he may realize for having encouraged me in graduate school to continue my interest in Joyce. A little later I could not have done without the expert guidance and generous enthusiasm of Professor James K. Robinson of the University of Cincinnati. The knowledgeability, advice, and firm encouragement of Professor Robert Scholes of Brown University over the past several years have been more than I could adequately acknowledge. Professor William Rueckert of the University of Rochester provided judgement and creative criticism at a time when I most needed them, and both he and his wife welcomed me then to their hospitable environment in Rochester.

My colleague, Professor Leon Waldoff, read this in manuscript form. His considerable learning in psychoanalytic literary criticism and his thoughtful suggestions were available to me at just the right time. For generosities too numerous to mention Professor Leonard Dean of New York University and Professor Sherman Paul of the University of Iowa deserve special gratitude. They cannot know how much I needed the encouragement and support they so generously and spontaneously provided. I must also thank Professor Lynn Altenbernd, Professor George Hendrick, and Dean Robert Rogers of the University of Illinois for their support and assistance. Professor William Curtin, of the University of Connecticut, Professor John Callahan of Lewis and Clark College, and Professor Michael Hollington of the University of East Anglia were tough, perceptive, and invariably constructive critics. Professor Hollington assisted me with reading Ferrero's book in Italian. My colleagues, Professors Paul Friedman and Mark Costello, and my officemate, Professor James Hurt have been gracious, perceptive, and encouraging. Also, I am most grateful to Professor Louis Fraiberg of the University of Toledo for having read this manuscript in final form. The enthusiasm for my work of Mr. Richard Wentworth of the University of Illinois Press has been truly gratifying.

Professor George Healey of Cornell University allowed me to examine at my leisure the material in the Cornell Joyce Collection. Miss Eva Benton and Mrs. Helen Welch of the magnificent University of Illinois Library have been gracious and helpful beyond the call of duty. And I thank the University of Chicago Library for efficient and generous assistance with interlibrary loan materials.

I am indebted to the Graduate Research Board of the University of Illinois for two Summer Faculty Fellowships to support this study. Also, the Research Committee of the Department of English of the University of Illinois has generously subsidized travel and typing expenses in connection with my work. I wish to thank Miss Beverly Seward for typing the manuscript in final form. Miss Martha Bergland of the University of Illinois Press has edited my manuscript with such a careful eye that any errors left in it can only be my own.

Finally I acknowledge with gratitude and affection the intelligence, assistance, encouragement, and criticism of my wife, Agnes McSharry Brandabur.

CONTENTS

	Introduction	3
CHAPTER I	The Green Stem of Fortune: Paralysis as Prospect	35
CHAPTER II	The Broken Harmonium: Paralysis as Celibacy	57
CHAPTER III	The Gratefully Oppressed: Paralysis as Humiliation	83
CHAPTER IV	"Ivy Day in the Committee Room" and "The Dead": Paralysis as Pretense	109
CHAPTER V	*Exiles*: A Rough and Tumble Between de Sade and Sacher-Masoch	127
CONCLUSION	*A Portrait of the Artist as a Young Man* and *Ulysses*	159
	Bibliography	175
	Index	181

A SCRUPULOUS MEANNESS

INTRODUCTION

THIS STUDY focuses on James Joyce's *Dubliners* and on *Exiles*, concluding with a brief commentary on the extent to which *A Portrait of the Artist as a Young Man* and *Ulysses* resolve the psychological malaise depicted in the earlier work. Throughout, I have imagined Joyce's characters as real and I have perceived what he was saying about them in the configurations of psychoanalysis. I do not psychoanalyse the Dubliners. Such is not possible with characters in fiction, even if one acquiesces in the author's illusion that they are real. Psychoanalysis requires a constant preoccupation with the patient's antecedent biography, the most revealing features of which he may have repressed. But characters in fiction exist entirely within a context imagined by the author, and particularly in his early work, Joyce provides little antecedent biography. In *A Portrait* and in *Ulysses*, he supplies Stephen and Bloom with a wealth of images and fantasies originating in the past to an extent never seen previously in literature. Nevertheless, as William Griffin has observed, "characters in a play, poem, or novel are of a different order of creation from those who may in the flesh consult the psychoanalyst."[1] Some of the most valid objections against the application of psychoanalytic insight to fiction arise from perceiving the neglect of this distinction.[2]

In the following study I do no more than to describe in analytic

[1] William J. Griffin, "The Use and Abuse of Psychoanalysis in the Study of Literature" in *Hidden Patterns: Studies in Psychoanalytic Literary Criticism*, ed. Leonard and Eleanor Manheim (New York, 1966), p. 26.

[2] Deploring unquestioned critical acquiescence in the illusion that literary characters have a life of their own, Griffin observes that, "the tenor of some psychoanalytic disquisitions suggests that more than one analyst may have in the works a volume on *The Infancy of Shakespeare's Heroes*." *Ibid.*, p. 25.

terms what Joyce has already depicted: the paralytic psychopathology of Dublin. Consequently, I have tried to avoid reading into the characters histories beyond what Joyce has given, though in a few instances psychoanalytic orthodoxy has obliged me to inference. Nevertheless, I have kept in mind Leon Edel's admonition: "Psychoanalysis, properly speaking, cannot be practiced upon inert materials; a living consciousness must be available, providing fantasy and rationalization, 'transference' and all the clinical evidence brought into a room by a physical presence."[3]

I wish to avoid reductive explication of the rich work of one of the greatest writers. From the start I assume Joyce's superior artistry and that his works no longer require the support of either defense or admiration. But precisely because of his artistic superiority, and because of the indisputable richness of his achievement, his work will always remain open to interpretation. Because this aspect has been neglected, I have chosen to perceive Joyce's work from a psychoanalytic perspective despite the risk of neglecting other aspects of his work. Nevertheless, I agree with William Phillips concerning the application of psychoanalytic criticism: "If art is considered as a form of sublimation, or a variety of dream or fantasy, or even as a therapeutic activity, then we have no criteria for judging it, nor any way of distinguishing it from other kinds of dream or fantasy, or therapy."[4] I do not regard Joyce's art as a form of sublimation, though he could hardly have avoided incidental sublimation in his work. I do not regard his art as a variety of dream or fantasy so much as I regard dream and fantasy as a form of art, less consciously so, perhaps, than the novel. However, one cannot deny that Joyce regarded his fiction as a diagnosis of his fellow Dubliners. We are on less certain grounds speculating about the extent to which Joyce diagnosed himself in his work. The evidence is inadequate.

[3] Leon Edel, "Notes on the Use of Psychological Tools in Literary Scholarship," *Newsletter of the Conference on Literature and Psychology of the Modern Language Association* 1 (September, 1951): 1.

[4] William Phillips, "Introduction: Art and Neurosis" in *Art and Psychoanalysis*, ed. William Phillips (Cleveland, 1967), p. xvi.

Lionel Trilling has expertly defused the notion that the chief factor in a work of art is the neurosis of its author, though he does not neglect the role that neurosis may play in the work of a given author.[5] In any case, psychoanalytic constructs have too often been used to explicate the author rather than his work, frequently an annoying process. My main purpose is not the explication of Joyce but of his work.[6]

A frequent tendency has been the psychoanalytic illumination of audience response to fiction, studied by critics such as Simon O. Lesser and Norman Holland.[7] I am not chiefly concerned here with this intriguing and worthwhile aspect of psychoanalytic criticism, though I will comment on it briefly after giving an opinion about the worth of psychoanalysis as a biographical method for Joyce.

Presumably, a thorough psychoanalytic biography of Joyce is possible, though without the living author to interrogate, highly improbable. It does not seem to me there is enough information. His letters to Nora are patently susceptible to psychoanalytic reading, but they issue from three brief periods of his life, and though indisputably informative, one could hardly base a thorough psychoanalytic biography on what they appear to reveal. Except for Joyce's letters to Nora, and perhaps a few to his brother Stanislaus, the three-volume collection of letters yields remarkably little psychoanalytically useful information. Even the definitive biography by Richard Ellmann was not constructed on psychoanalytic assumptions, though without the conditioning of Freud

[5] Lionel Trilling, "Art and Neurosis" in *ibid.*, pp. 502–520.

[6] Norman Holland has thoroughly discussed the options available to a psychoanalytic critic, as well as the hazards implicit in each option, in "Shakespearean Tragedy and the Three Ways of Psychoanalytic Criticism" in *Psychoanalysis and Literature*, ed. Hendrik M. Ruitenbeek (New York, 1964), pp. 207–217. I have chosen the second option, relating Joyce's fiction to the minds of his characters, rather than to the minds of either Joyce or his audience. This same approach, says Holland, has been most frequently taken, at least with Shakespearean tragedy.

[7] Simon O. Lesser's pioneer study, *Fiction and the Unconscious* (New York, 1962), is indispensable. Norman Holland's *The Dynamics of Literary Response* (New York, 1968) supplements Lesser.

Ellmann might have been silent about the ambivalences operating in his subject. It remains that Joyce lives in his work, transformed into his own artifact. No method has been devised which could extract him from his work, nor, I think, is such a method likely. Despite Jung's observation that the sublimation of his art saved Joyce from the tragic fate of his daughter Lucia[8]—an observation impossible to verify—my own opinion is that for the most part one should avoid psychoanalyzing Joyce through his work. One is more certain in the application of analytic concepts to the characters in his work. His legacy to us is not himself but his work.

That fiction satisfies the universal human desire for vicarious participation, making good "the deficiencies of experience," forms the subject of Simon O. Lesser's *Fiction and the Unconscious*. Lesser demonstrates how fiction gratifies human need by evoking in its readers not merely a cognitive response, but a participation in "the events it sets before us." In his view, fiction "offers us not simply a spectacle but an experience."[9] For Lesser catharsis is the therapeutic function of fiction: "It permits a discharge of feeling which is very real though it is based on imaginary fulfillment."[10] Thus he agrees with Aristotle's basic insight in *The Poetics* that works of fiction, particularly the tragic, operate as safety valves for "humanity's over-repressed instincts."[11] Up to a point this notion is reasonable enough, though in my view it will not sufficiently explain the way people employ vicarious experience in life for manipulation and control. Lesser's book concentrates almost exclusively on the normal response to fiction, whereas throughout this study I stress basically pathological, manipulative uses of vi-

---

[8] Because he could creatively "will" his own schizophrenic style, rather than (as with the ordinary schizophrenic) be passively subject to the illness, Joyce "did not go over the border." But, Jung wrote, "His daughter did, because she was no genius like her father, but merely a victim of her disease." Richard Ellmann, *James Joyce* (New York, 1959), p. 692.

[9] Lesser, *Fiction and the Unconscious*, p. 238.

[10] *Ibid.*, p. 254.

[11] *Ibid.*

carious experience. Of course, Lesser is concerned with reader response and I am concerned with the depiction of the vicarious response of *characters* towards other characters. Nevertheless, I think Lesser devotes insufficient attention to the way in which both conscious and unconscious response to fiction may, if pathological, serve to gratify a reader's repressed wish for sadomasochistic control of himself and others through participation in imaginary experience. Furthermore, he does not indicate that often fiction criticises its own function as the gratification of vicarious experience. This autocriticism is a factor in the rise of the so-called anti-novel, which in one sense may be defined as an artistic response to the opportunity for vicarious experience that fiction makes available. For example, *Don Quixote* is an archetypal anti-novel, and many subsequent authors have followed Cervantes's pattern of ironically portraying experience which is a response to the nature of fiction as a form of vicarious experience. "There is," writes Jean Rousset, "an anti-novel when the novel has a bad conscience, when it turns critical and autocritical and breaks with the existent novel."[12]

When readers incline to accept as real the vicarious experience in fiction, novelists will dramatize the distinction between second- and firsthand experience. Flaubert's *Madame Bovary* is an anti-novel for its criticism of the effect on Emma of having taken the vicarious experience in provincial lending libraries for her reality. As Enid Starkie has observed:

> [Emma] has no positive character herself, but sees herself in various parts, at different times—as the great lover, the devoted mother, the mystic—and all these parts are built up artificially and are inspired by her reading of romantic novels, so that she is incapable of living life directly, but only through some fanciful idea. From her reading she took only what could be incorporated into her picture of herself. The literature of the time encouraged this concentra-

[12] Jean Rousset, "*Madame Bovary* or the Book about Nothing" in *Flaubert: A Collection of Critical Essays*, ed. Raymond Giraud (Englewood Cliffs, N.J., 1964), p. 112.

tion on self and she borrowed from it only what could feed this obsession.[13]

At the same time, of course, one may perceive *Madame Bovary* as a criticism of that male chauvinism implicit in Charles, who cannot create appropriate circumstances for his wife's real satisfaction. Without imagination and therefore incapable himself of vicarious experience, Charles Bovary becomes part of a fantasy the reader can oppose by identification with Emma. Yet, Charles emerges capable of sympathy, Emma emerges selfish, imprisoned by her own narcissism. *Madame Bovary* was both novel and anti-novel.

Compulsively literal characters, such as Akaky in Gogol's *The Overcoat* and Dostoevsky's Raskolnikov, avoided fiction, but were inclined to act out what they had absorbed from their mad involvement with the textual. Their inclinations to live out the letter of the document corresponded to those of lovers of fiction to live within the imaginative experience they had read about. Frequently, the clerk, the attorney, the scribe, the bureaucrat, and the cleric of nineteenth-century literature were neurotic literalists with an urge to make real their experience of the letter. Tolstoy perceived the extent to which this compulsive one-dimensionality could cover up the reality of self-insight. His pompous judge in "The Death of Ivan Ilych" is on the verge of salvation only when pain lures him from behind his image as an authoritarian, desk-bound literalist:

> He would say to himself: 'I will take up my duties again—*after all I used to live by them*' [italics mine]. And banishing all doubts he would go to the law courts, enter into conversation with his colleagues, and sit carelessly as was his wont, scanning the crowd with a thoughtful look and leaning both his emaciated arms on the arms of his oak chair. . . but suddenly, in the midst of those proceedings the pain in his side, regardless of the stage the proceedings had reached, would begin its own gnawing work. Ivan Ilych would

[13] Enid Starkie, *Flaubert: The Making of the Master* (New York, 1967), p. 318.

turn his attention to it and try to drive the thought of it away, but without success. *It* would come and stand before him and look at him, and he would be petrified and the light would die out of his eyes, and he would again begin asking himself whether *It* alone was true. And his colleagues and subordinates would see with surprise and distress that he, the brilliant and subtle judge, was becoming confused and making mistakes.[14]

Joyce's James Duffy, in "A Painful Case," and his Father Flynn, in "The Sisters," are in the same line, paralysed morally by attempting to live according to books thick with inhuman proscriptions. Unlike Tolstoy's Ivan Ilych, they do not achieve the salvation of honesty.

In the novel itself, the lover of vicarious experience through fiction has often been either a woman or a student, presumably because since they had leisure to read "for amusement," fiction could make up for the privation of "real" experience resulting from their roles, outside the current of what men of affairs regard as "life." Stendhal's Julian Sorel, Flaubert's Emma, are prime examples, their misfortunes being in part the result of excess affection for the "reality" of vicarious experience.

Huysmans's Des Esseintes could eventually live entirely by means of mechanical surrogate experience. The conjunction of personal wealth with late nineteenth-century technological achievement permitted him to substitute secondhand experience for real experience. He no longer required the novel, dreaming instead of a hermitage "equipped with all the modern conveniences," capable of satisfying his desire for controllable experience. One by one he rejected conventional satisfactions, eventually refusing to mix with "young men of his own age and society." He spurned women of high and low degree, and even "men of letters," though at first he had imagined these were "kindred spirits." Intensely neurotic, Des Esseintes found "real" experience tedious and repugnant. He dis-

[14] Leo Tolstoy, "The Death of Ivan Ilych" in *The Death of Ivan Ilych and Other Stories*, trans. Aylmer Maude (New York, 1960), pp. 132–133.

missed as "irrelevant" even the conventional forms of surrogate satisfaction—literature, art, scholarship, the brothel, all of which had served wealthy escapists in simpler times.

The chief requirement of Des Esseintes's suburban Eden was that it should fulfill his wish to be "any where out of the world," in the title of a prose poem he likes.[15] He pays close attention to the achievements of an age in which mechanical brides were actually possible. Nature having "had her day," woman, deemed the "most perfect and original beauty"[16] of Nature could no longer match the locomotive:

> Does there exist, anywhere on this earth, a being conceived in the joys of fornication and born in the throes of motherhood who is more dazzlingly, more outstandingly beautiful than the two loco-motives recently put into service on the Northern Railway?. . . One of these, bearing the name of Crampton, is an adorable blonde with a shrill voice, a long slender body imprisoned in a shiny brass corset, and supple catlike movements; a smart golden blonde whose extraordinary grace can be quite terrifying when she stiffens her muscles of steel, sends the sweat pouring down her steaming flanks, sets her elegant wheels spinning in their wide circles, and hurtles away, full of life, at the head of an express or a boat-train. . . . The other, Engerth by name, is a strapping saturnine brunette given to uttering raucous, guttural cries, with a thick-set figure encased in armour-plating of cast iron; a monstrous creature with her di-shevelled mane of black smoke and her six wheels coupled together low down, she gives an indication of her fantastic strength when, with an effort that shakes the very earth, she slowly and deliberately drags along her heavy train of goods-wagons. . . . It is beyond ques-tion that, among all the fair, delicate beauties and all the dark, ma-jestic charmers of the human race, no such superb examples of comely grace and terrifying force are to be found; and it can be stated without fear of contradiction that in his chosen province man has done as well as the God in whom he believes.[17]

[15] J. K. Huysmans, *Against Nature*, trans. Robert Baldick (Baltimore, 1959), p. 31.
[16] *Ibid.*, p. 37.
[17] *Ibid.*, pp. 37–38.

This remarkable, ironic admiration for the mechanical bride marks the end of that series of fatal women who had previously served the neurotic experience of fiction. No longer are they even imagined as real women. The erotic locomotives, Crampton and Engerth, sum up with mechanical perfection the light-haired, aristocratic, catlike hauteur, and the dark-haired, guttural brutality of a thousand fictional heroines. Crampton and Engerth include the angelic, cloacal; shrill, raucous; slender, thickset; elegant, vulgar; civilized, wild. For Des Esseintes, they satisfy a compulsion to feel himself into sadomasochistic extremes of power and submission through his orgiastic adoration of the mechanism. His enthusiasm issues from a recognition of the power of mechanism to replace conventional fictional mimesis as a means of the vicarious experience of triumph and abasement. Thus, his wish represented the quintessence of mechanistic vicarious experiencing. This technology would come to be outdated in turn by the prospect of electronic vicarious experiencing prophesied in the telegraphic fantasies of Leopold Bloom and culminating in the magnificent insight of William Burroughs, whose *Naked Lunch* portrays a terminal stage in human surrogate experience permitted by a merger of electricity and heroin. In a sense, Huysmans's novel initiates contemporary fiction, just as it terminates nineteenth-century fiction. "All the prose works of the Decadence are contained in embryo in *A Rebours*," wrote Mario Praz.[18]

The ideal "women" in *Against Nature* are relatives of Sacher-Masoch's Wanda of *Venus in Furs*, and De Sade's Eugenie in *Philosophy in the Bedroom*, not to mention the multitude of fictional sinister women catalogued by Mario Praz in *The Romantic Agony*. However, the erotic locomotives are greatly more responsive to neurotic obsession than their fictional cousins because they are not organic. "Controlling" them in fantasy requires neither the progressive education of Wanda's sensibility achieved by Sacher-Masoch's

[18] Mario Praz, *The Romantic Agony*, trans. Angus Davidson (New York, 1951), p. 309.

Severin, nor the elaborate rules and spintrian acrobatics of De Sade's Madame de Saint Ange and the Chevalier de Mirvel. Once put together Crampton and Engerth need only a hand on the onanistic throttle. "Instant women," they were in their time smooth models for vicarious neurotic experience—efficient engines for immediate power and immediate humiliation. Huysmans could not yet tune in on the radio-television fantasies subsequently assembled by western technology.

Nevertheless, *Against Nature* prepared the way for works like *Dubliners, Exiles,* and particularly *Ulysses,* all of which are intricate descriptions of primarily masculine fantasy life. Within those elaborate fantasies, the wish is constantly present for instant control by means of neurotic manipulation of the feminine or feminized source of pleasure, often by an imagined participation in frequently humiliating and degrading erotic experience. The erotic gratification Bloom perceived in Gerty MacDowell and Joyce epitomized in Molly Bloom is as much at the demand of aesthetically sublimated masculine tyranny as those remarkable sexual locomotives Des Esseintes admired, though Leopold Bloom both is and is not his descendent, just as the reality of Molly Bloom exceeds that of Huysmans's fictional iron women.[19]

In its perpetual autocriticism the novel resembles psychoanalysis, which implants in the patient an autocriticism of his own fantasy, his own preference for the surrogate pleasure of vicarious experience in place of the frequent pain of real experience. Though it is many other things as well, fiction is a form of vicarious psychoanalysis. A constant theme in the following study will be the extent to which Joyce, a master of the fictional mode, was thoroughly involved in the process of anti-fiction. In this process he had many great predecessors. Much in the manner of his predecessors, Joyce

[19] A precise analysis of the role of masculine erotic fantasy, particularly in modern fiction, is found in Kate Millet's essay "Sexual Politics: Miller, Mailer, and Genet," *New American Review* 7, ed. Theodore Solotaroff (New York, 1969), pp. 7–31.

was somewhat aware of his own propensities for vicarious gratification of the general masculine wish for sadomasochistic vicarious
experience, although as I have indicated one has only the intimate
evidence from brief periods of his life to go on, and must hesitate
to make sweeping psychoanalytic generalizations about his whole
character. Consequently I have seldom deciphered his personality
from studying his work. Where biography and letters illuminate the
work I have used them, but not primarily for an understanding of
Joyce the man. It is necessary to modify this resolution briefly to
describe the attitude he held towards his subject matter—that is
towards Dublin, and to indicate with deliberate sketchiness something of the psychosexual implications of that attitude.

He wanted to give his compatriots a good look at themselves in
his "nicely polished looking-glass,"[20] ostensibly so they would not
shun the therapy of self-awareness. But ruthlessly he subjected
them to his own contempt. "I feel the day all wasted here among the
common Dublin people whom I hate and despise,"[21] he wrote to
Nora. In another letter he said: "I loathe Ireland and the Irish.
They themselves stare at me in the street though I was born among
them. Perhaps they read my hatred of them in my eyes."[22] It is
worth noting that at times Joyce also betrayed moderate affection
for his city, though this seems to me largely retrospective. In focus
here is the attitude he revealed while composing most of the stories
in *Dubliners,* a time of great personal strain and frustration. Writing about "The Dead," Richard Ellmann noted Joyce's feeling that
"the rest of the stories in *Dubliners* had not completed his picture
of the city. In a letter of September 25, 1906, he had written his
brother from Rome to say that some elements of Dublin had been
left out of his stories: 'I have not reproduced its ingenuous insularity and its hospitality, the latter "virtue" so far as I can see does

[20] Joyce to Grant Richards, 23 June 1906, *Letters,* vol. 1, ed. Stuart Gilbert
(New York, 1966), p. 64.
[21] Joyce to Nora, 25 October 1909, *Letters,* vol. 2, ed. Richard Ellmann (New
York, 1966), p. 254.
[22] Joyce to Nora, 27 October 1909, *Letters,* vol. 2, p. 255.

not exist elsewhere in Europe.' He allowed a little of this warmth to enter 'The Dead.' "[23]

Even a temporary hatred was an understandable if not completely just response. At this time Joyce was sick of Dublin, "the city of failure, of rancour and of unhappiness."[24] However, limited by hatred, a writer's point of view may also be aesthetically narrow. Even Joyce's comic vision does not diminish his loathing so much as it makes it less painful for him to bear.

By contrast, Flaubert approached the French bourgeoisie from the limited perspective of contempt, but his final sympathies were as large as life. The role of hater was too small for him. Contemptible from Emma's point of view, Charles Bovary becomes heroic when seen from that of Flaubert because Flaubert's point of view both includes and transcends contempt. He transforms our sympathy for Emma to an awareness of her self-deception.

Though displaying an ironical vision of human life, Flaubert would not permit himself total immersion in irony. As Mary McCarthy has observed, "Flaubert's ironies are deceptive, and what sounds like irony is often a simple truth, making a double irony."[25] The simple truth Flaubert expressed, according to his biographer, Enid Starkie, was "sorrow and pity for man, his condition; not criticism of what he is or does, but compassion for what he is called upon to endure."[26] This attitude transcends both irony and sentimentality and thus is more humane than that of the apprentice Joyce, though in *Ulysses* the Joycean attitude would come to resemble that of Flaubert. After all, Joyce assured us of his compassionate affection for Bloom. Through the gentle light of this affection, however tempered by a scrupulous cunning, one perceives

[23] Ellmann, *James Joyce*, p. 254.

[24] Joyce to Nora, 22 August 1909, *Letters*, vol. 2, p. 239.

[25] Mary McCarthy, foreword to *Madame Bovary* (New York, 1964), p. xxii. Her view is that, "Charles is the hero of the book that, characteristically for him, bears someone else's name."

[26] Starkie, *Flaubert*, p. 333.

the humblest Dubliner in *Ulysses* softened by time and distance. *Ulysses* has little of the rancor apparent in *Dubliners*. In *A Portrait of the Artist*, Joyce began the liberation of his own alter ego. In *Ulysses* he began to free his compatriots, if only from his own inchoate perception. In *A Portrait*, this process led to the more individualized captivity of a unique role. *Ulysses* describes a disillusionment with this unique captivity of the artist-hero.[27]

Resembling the Dubliners he shrewdly portrayed, Joyce seemed a master of poses, to Nora at least a confessed imposter: "How is it that I cannot impress you with my magnificent poses as I do other people? You see through me, you cunning little blue-eyed rogue, and smile to yourself knowing that I am an imposter and still you love me."[28] By this rule, even his intimate letters to Nora, and his outspokenness to Stanislaus are suspect. His admissions of imposture were strategic. Frequently they were to mollify Nora and should be taken as affectations of humility. Usually, he contradicted his self-accusations, at times in the same letter. In the letter just quoted, he prefaces his "admission" of deceitfulness with the assertion that, "I am not a bad man. I am a poor impulsive sinful generous dissatisfied kind-natured poet but I am not a bad deceitful person."[29] In the same sentence he denies the meanness he admits. Then, he denies deceitfulness and, in the next sentence, admits he is deceitful. One can take him at his word only when he admits behavior he demonstrates.

In an earlier letter to Nora he had written: "Can you not see the simplicity which is at the back of all my disguises? We all wear

[27] In a letter to Stanislaus, Joyce condemned "the whole structure of heroism" as "a damned lie." He apparently had in mind the notion of the hero as one who sacrificed himself for a group. Instead, Joyce felt that, "there cannot be any substitute for the individual passion as the motive power of everything— art and philosophy included." 7 February 1905, *Letters*, vol. 2, p. 81. This statement appears to have summarized the concept of heroism actually employed in his early work, especially in *Stephen Hero*, *A Portrait*, and *Exiles*.

[28] Joyce to Nora, 25 December 1909, *Letters*, vol. 2, p. 279.

[29] *Ibid.*, pp. 278–279.

masks."[30] Of course, we wonder what was this "simplicity" behind the disguises? What was the Joycean self? It does not seem enough to define this self as the one who juggled all the masques. Yet, though preferring a more definitive notion, we must, I think, remain content with the little Joyce revealed. Not surprisingly, the letters to Nora in the Cornell library demonstrate somewhat the connection between Joyce's fiction and his own lively and apparently compulsive fantasy life: that is to say between his work and a personal neurosis defined in the deliberately limited, chiefly functional sense employed throughout this study. As it operates in Joyce's Dublin, neurosis appears to have a clearly sadomasochistic character, expressed in relationships where there is a demonstrable and recurrent compulsion to restore a diminished sense of power and control through posing and mimicry. In this way, the universal experience of neurosis is given individuation in the works of Joyce. Within this functional meaning of neurosis, the symptoms are chiefly poses juggled by a single self, implying a diminished confidence in the "real" self. A masterful if somewhat transparent juggler, Joyce was himself the simplicity behind his disguises. But unlike his fellow Dubliners, he managed to articulate a stunning sense of inner definition, chiefly perhaps because he had the consolation of his artistry.

In his letters to Nora, he wishes to use her in a drama of power. She will play the maternal tormentor with himself in a masochistic role. He would displease her so that cane in hand she might call him into the room her face deep red with anger. She would point to what he had done, throw him face downward on her lap, tear off his clothes while he struggled helplessly, and then flog him viciously on his naked "quivering" flesh.[31] At another time he wishes to live in her womb: "My little mother, take me into the dark sanctuary of your womb. Shelter me, dear, from harm! I am too childish and impulsive to live alone. Help me, dear, pray for me! Love me!

[30] Joyce to Nora, 29 August 1904, *Letters*, vol. 2, p. 49.
[31] Joyce to Nora, 7 December 1909, Item 243 in Cornell Joyce Collection.

Think of me! I am so helpless tonight, helpless, helpless!"[32] One perceives, however, that it was always Joyce himself who was in control.

The sadistic face of Joyce's sadomasochistic inclination appears in his compulsion to imagine Nora's degradation. He contemplates intercourse with her while she defecates, grunting slowly like a a sow.[33] He thinks of her as a prostitute, "half-naked and obscene."[34]

The acting out in fantasy of sadomasochistic postures, with Nora prancing in his imagination, connects with Joyce's juggling the spiritual and the sensual in his poetic role. He perceived in himself an unstable composition of artistry with less exalted elements he viewed with a mixture of dismay and indulgence. The bestial made way for the spiritual or poetic. Deploring to Nora the "obscene and filthy" sexual acts he had written her about, he felt in retrospect they constituted "a moment of brutal madness."[35] Nevertheless, he concludes, when the sexual act is over (from this letter it appears he masturbated along with the fantasies he describes), "a faint hymn is heard rising in tender worship from the dim cloisters of [my] heart."[36]

One imagines Joyce in a monastery adjoining the dung-spread farm which nourishes the monks for their liturgy. Behind each psalm is the energy of bovine faeces and pig-sty rutting. His art required a gross liaison with Nora which his own words describe as lustful, brutish, filthy, and obscene. Though in spiritual moments he preferred to look away from the barnyard, at other times he revelled in its life. Often, this life teemed even in the mind's eye of the monk at prayer. Inside his spiritual affection for Nora, he wrote, was "a wild beast-like craving" for her body.[37] His monastic

[32] Joyce to Nora, 24 December 1909, *Letters*, vol. 2, p. 281.

[33] Joyce to Nora, 16 December 1909, Item 262 in Cornell Joyce Collection.

[34] Joyce to Nora, 2 September 1909, *Letters*, vol. 2, p. 243.

[35] Joyce to Nora, 2 December 1909, *Letters*, vol. 2, p. 269.

[36] Joyce to Nora, 1 (or 2) December 1909, Item 250 in Cornell Joyce Collection.

[37] Joyce to Nora, 2 December 1909, *Letters*, vol. 2, p. 269.

role inclined him to visit shrines. Tears in his eyes, he kneels by Nora's bed on a visit to Ireland, like the magi.[38] The self, the "simplicity behind the masks" projected a sadist and a masochist, a beast and a monk. But he was aware of his sadism and masochism, yearning to fashion himself in a different image, as the quest for liberation in the autobiographical *Portrait* implies.

In the tedious inhumanity of Dublin, Joyce also saw unsavory elements. But between himself and his characters exists the distinction of self-awareness. Ordinarily, the Dubliners suffer as captives of a pose they have long since forgotten was a pose. The pose is a normal condition of life. They refuse to question this condition because they cannot renounce the delight they take in their subjection to imposture. Thus they are spiritually moribund. At the same time he rejoices in his own posing, Joyce is quick to its horror, as he will suggest in *A Portrait of the Artist* and as he will proclaim through the comedy of *Ulysses*.

Despite his attitude towards Dublin, I have assumed that Joyce's work was sufficiently detached from him to disclose relatively little disguised information about himself, but a good deal about Dublin. He thought himself a consciousness of his race, and we should take him at his word. Though there was much of which his Dubliners were unaware, there was little in them to which Joyce was blind. He may have been unaware of much in himself, though little of this appears in his work. He was more acutely alive and conscious in his work than in his life.

I do not imply that Joyce had an openly psychoanalytical perception, or that he would have described his work in the terms I use. My presumption is in the bearing of psychoanalytic concepts on the work of an author who was not indoctrinated with them, however intimately he knew the activities they describe. I take comfort in a statement by Thomas Mann, several years after he wrote *The Magic Mountain*:

[38] Joyce to Nora, 11 December 1909, *Letters*, vol. 2, p. 273.

I have been much helped by foreign criticism and I consider it a mistake to think that the author himself is the best judge of his work. He may be that while he is still at work on it and living in it. But once done, it tends to be something he has got rid of, something foreign to him; others, as time goes on, will know more and better about it than he. They can often remind him of things in it he has forgotten or indeed quite never knew. . . . Our consciousness is feeble; only in moments of unusual clarity and vision do we really know about ourselves. As for me, I am glad to be instructed by critics about myself, to learn from them about my past works and go back to them in my mind.[39]

It is difficult to imagine Joyce responding to literary criticism with Mann's aristocratic grace. Very likely, he would have reacted to recent studies of his work, including my own, with irony or resentment. Nevertheless, perhaps I am one of those who have become equipped in time to "know more and better about it" than Joyce himself. I would preface a further justification for my method with another quotation from Thomas Mann:

The analytic revelation is a revolutionary force. With it a blithe skepticism has come into the world, a mistrust which unmasks all the schemes and subterfuges of our own souls. Once roused and on the alert, it cannot be put to sleep again. It infiltrates life, undermines its raw naïevté, takes from it the strain of its own ignorance, deemotionalizes it, as it were, inculcates the taste for understatement. . . for the deflated rather than for the inflated word, for the cult which exerts its influence by moderation.[40]

Probably it is true that, especially in his early work, Joyce was little influenced by the particular "analytic revelation" initiated by

[39] Thomas Mann, "The Making of *The Magic Mountain*" in *The Magic Mountain* (New York, 1953), p. 725.

[40] Thomas Mann, "Freud and the Future" in *Art and Psychoanalysis*, ed. Phillips, p. 388. By way of further justification for the method I employ, I should mention particularly Frederick Crews's essay on "Literature and Psychology" in the MLA pamphlet, *Relations of Literary Study* (New York, 1967), pp. 73–87. Crews writes, "Psychoanalysis is the only psychology to have seriously altered our way of reading literature" (p. 73).

Freud. Later, in *Ulysses*, his Stephen Dedalus deliberately opposes his own "Thomistic" version of incest to that of "The New Viennese School."[41] A familiar pun in *Finnegans Wake*, about " 'alices" being "yung and easily freudened," indicates his final attitude towards psychoanalysis to be a kind of parody. Nevertheless, the shrewd and complex attitude Joyce held towards all the characters in his fiction—even towards his *alter ego*, Stephen—implies a scepticism resembling that Mann attributed to the revolutionary perception spawned by Freudian analysis. Wishing to "betray" the soul of his own city, Joyce unmasked the schemes and subterfuges of Dublin; infiltrating its life, his eye undermined the raw naïveté of ordinary perception, at the same time maintaining almost everywhere an understated tone, deflating the Aeolian windbag of Dublin rhetoric, swelled with enthymeme. Surely it would be claiming too much on little direct evidence that Joyce was working within a frame of perception equivalent to that of Freud. But it seems to me that the subtle analyses of human character in Joyce shared in that remarkable revolution in human personal and social perception begun by Freud and his contemporaries. For reasons possibly unfathomable, Joyce was able to emerge from the pit of the Irish unconscious and see his environment as no one had seen it. This unconscious, epitomized in *A Portrait* by the old peasant with "red-rimmed, horny eyes," became a force to struggle against—a force preferring the cavern to the light. "With him I must struggle all through this night till day come, till he or I lie dead."[42] Battle with a demonic racial unconscious can only be waged by weapons

[41] In one of the most rewarding applications of psychoanalytic theory to literature I have read, William Wasserstrom notes that despite Joyce's denial of psychoanalytic influence, "he was better informed in these matters than he liked to admit." But, "he sought out not the obvious but the recondite, not Freud but Otto Rank with whom he seems to share some special attitudes on language, myth, art, and artists." "In Gertrude's Closet: Incest-Patterns in Recent Literature" in Manheim, *Hidden Patterns*, p. 285.

[42] Joyce, *A Portrait of the Artist as a Young Man* (New York, 1966), p. 252. All subsequent references to *A Portrait* will be from this text, page numbers to be indicated in parentheses after the quotation.

fashioned in the shop of insight and perception, under conditions described as silence, exile, and cunning. Silence implies the most favorable circumstance for a diagnostic ear; exile, a necessary distance; cunning, the prerequisite for discrimination between perverse and benign motivations. These were precisely the conditions in which Freud worked, just as insight and perception constituted his own inner strength. It seems to me one should not restrict the notion of "analytic revelation" to Freudian analysis, but must enlarge it to include the temper of this age. Joyce partook of that spirit of intellectual revolution of which psychoanalysis was a most obtrusive manifestation. Along with his subtle analyses of human character, he assisted in the dismantling of a hitherto unquestioned counter-reformation synthesis still operative in backwater Ireland long after the children of rationalism had dismantled it elsewhere. No one can be unaware that with *Ulysses* Joyce took apart, perhaps fractured, the aesthetic synthesis achieved in the nineteenth-century novel—the notion of a secure point of view on which the novel had come to rest. The justification for approaching Joyce from a psychoanalytical perspective is that, though he was seldom explicitly psychoanalytical, his perceptions of human character proceed out of the same sceptical, analytic perception, the same urge to unmask generated by European rationalism, which nurtured the perception of the "New Viennese School." That Joycean and Freudian visions should prove congruent in so many respects serves chiefly to establish the validity of their shrewd insights about human character, the efficacy of what Mann called, "a mistrust which unmasks all the schemes and subterfuges of our own souls."

As Joyce admitted, his insight into the human meanness in Dublin derived in part from a similar attitude in himself. While writing *Dubliners* he said in a letter to his brother: "Give me for Christ's sake a pen and an ink bottle and some peace of mind and then, by the crucified Jaysus, if I don't sharpen that little pen and dip it in fermented ink and write tiny little sentences about the people who

betrayed me and sent me to hell."[43] He described the human meanness of Dublin in a style of "scrupulous meanness,"[44] because such
a style was appropriate to his subject, the pettiness of human character, and because his attitude was often contemptuous, despite his
wish to modify this tone in "The Dead."[45] His style served as a
medium of expression and as a method of attitude control. Joyce
finally adopted a comic detachment. Whatever his personal feeling
towards Ireland, his deepest instincts urged laughter.

Dubliners portrays a subtle obstinacy Joyce called "paralysis,"
the sickness he saw infecting every feature of Dublin life.[46] This
paralysis amounts to a reluctance to be thoroughly human, in such
mean ways that "meanness" is more apt a name for how the Dubliners behave than "evil." This meanness takes a sadomasochistic
form. Though the term "sadomasochism" usually evokes images of
exotic perversity, in Joyce's Dublin it ordinarily operates as described on the first page of *Dubliners*: "[the word 'paralysis'] filled
me with fear, and yet I longed to be nearer to it and to look upon
its deadly work" (p. 9). These words from "The Sisters" sound a
dominant theme. They foreshadow the phenomenon Joyce portrays of vicarious experiencing or "feeling into" the ordinarily
humiliating but occasionally triumphant experience of others.
According to Wilhelm Stekel, this phenomenon unites sadism and
masochism in the disease of sadomasochism:

---

[43] Joyce to Stanislaus Joyce, about 24 September 1905, *Letters*, vol. 2, p. 110.

[44] Joyce to Grant Richards, 5 May 1906, *Letters*, vol. 2, p. 134.

[45] In his chapter from the biography of Joyce, on backgrounds of "The
Dead," Richard Ellmann points out that Joyce tried to atone for his harsh
portrayal of the Dubliners in the earlier stories by praising Dublin's hospitality
in "The Dead." Ellmann, *James Joyce*, pp. 252, 254, 263. Ellmann's view dis-
regards the irony in the story. For example, Gabriel Conroy remarks, "It is
not the first time that we have been the recipients—or perhaps, I had better
say, the victims—of the hospitality of certain good ladies." Joyce, *Dubliners*
(New York, 1967), p. 202. Subsequent page references to *Dubliners* will be from
this recently revised and now definitive edition.

[46] In a 1904 letter to Constantine Curran about his stories he wrote, "I call
the series *Dubliners* to betray the soul of that hemiplegia or paralysis which
many consider a city." n.d., *Letters*, vol. 1, p. 55.

An erroneous conception of the sado-masochistic complex makes pain the central factor for consideration and occupies itself with the phenomenon of gratification derived from pain . . . however . . . the decisive thing in the phenomenon of sado-masochism is the affect, which is fed from two sources: in the sadist, from his own sense of power in overcoming the resistance of another and from his feeling himself into the humiliation of his partner; in the masochist, from the overcoming of his own resistances (power over himself) and the feeling of himself into the partner who humbles him . . . we have not to do with separate events, but with polar expressions of a single complex.[47]

Feeling into the experience of others constitutes much of the paralysis Joyce said centered in Dublin, which is not to deny that the spiritual paralysis Joyce describes has other manifestations and stems from several causes. One cannot reduce the malaise of Dublin to a single source. However, I explicate the psychopathology of Joyce's Dublin because it is most in need of explication.

Perceiving that Joyce depicted his Dubliners as neurotic implies the application of some concept of the normal, though I am aware of the hazards implicit in such a conception. But I have found useful the criteria of "normality" outlined in Ernest Jones's essay, "The Concept of a Normal Mind."[48] Jones thought that the desired concept of normality would include happiness, efficiency in mental functioning, and positive social-feeling relationship. He defined happiness as a combination of the capacity for enjoyment with self-content, efficiency in mental functioning as the unimpeded flow of energy in the pursuit of any activity. The third element, "positive social-feeling relationship," required a free internal potential for feelings of sincere friendliness and affection. Underlying these is what he called the "nearest attainable criterion of normality," *angstfrei*, or fearlessness: "we must be clear that we mean by this not merely manifest courage, but the absence of all the deep re-

[47] Wilhelm Stekel, *Sadism and Masochism: The Psychology of Hatred and Cruelty*, trans. Louise Brink (New York, 1963), vol. 1, p. 57.

[48] Ernest Jones, "The Concept of a Normal Mind" in *Papers on Psychoanalysis* (Boston, 1961), pp. 201–216.

actions that mask unconscious apprehensiveness. Where these are absent we have the willing or even joyful acceptance of life, with all its visitations and chances, that distinguishes the free personality of one who is master of himself."[49] Though one might go on to develop a more sophisticated set of criteria for "normality," it is enough here to observe that the concepts at work in Joyce's mind resemble the more technical criteria of Jones. From the few remarks Joyce made about what he expected us to see in the mirror he held up to the soul of a city, it is clear that in his mind the Dubliners deviated from a human norm: Dublin was a city of "failure, of rancour, and of unhappiness." His compatriots were paralyzed, their psychic and emotional energies unavailable for constructive activity. Constantly, in his fiction and letters he castigates their incapacity for true friendship, their predilection for betrayal, their pathological conversion of affection into contempt, of eros into neurotic prudery. They were incapable of self-content, creative activity, sincere friendship, and affection. Furthermore, his stories consistently portray a national character undermined by both conscious and unconscious apprehensiveness about every feature of human existence—sexual, political, economic, religious, intellectual. If there is one constant emotion in Joyce's Dublin it is fear. Living in the debasement and in the triumph of others flows from and contributes to this paralysis of vital function in Dublin. Psychologically, Joyce's city was a closed and balanced system. But all fiction describes and evokes a "feeling into" the experience of others, though it is not always sadomasochistic nor does all literature have this "feeling into" as a pervasive theme. The work of Joyce is permeated with this theme. In her monologue, Molly consistently feels herself into the erotic experience of various men. Throughout his famous day, Leopold Bloom lives vicariously the experience of others—men and women. Incidentally, Joyce's letters to Nora frequently recount his wish to live her sexual experience in his imagination.

[49] *Ibid.*, p. 215.

The phenomena of vicarious experience and emphatic response follow from the mimetic character of fiction, though both the motivations and the special forms of vicarious experience differ among authors and within the works of Joyce himself. The evocation of nonpathological vicarious experience and empathetic response is distinct from the evocation of experience which defines sadomasochism. Intrinsic to this distinction is the element of neurotic pretense. Aristotle perceived the Athenians in open empathy with tragic figures, a response which implies the absence of pretense and secrecy. Aristotle was not aware of concealed smiles in the tragic humiliation of the mighty. Unconcealed laughter was left for comedy.

One cannot sympathize with the petty viciousness of Joyce's Dubliners. Laughter is more appropriate. Indeed the stories became more humorous as Joyce finally arranged them,[50] though the humor is chiefly ironic. We are ever conscious of looking upon a scene of bondage and frustration. Superior to the fictional environment we seem to have little part in it, and therefore we may feel minimal compassion in proportion to our great aesthetic distance. But if we are conscious of these elements, of what are we unconscious? Here, our own sham comes into play. Certainly the great appeal of *Dubliners* implies that Joyce's Dublin is a microcosm of our own world.

In Joyce's stories, theatre and audience are indistinct. The distance has dissolved which separated Athenians from the stage and made them aware they were not witnessing their own fate except in imagination. Within Joyce's stories, characters stage petty dramas of betrayal and frustration in which they delight in the discomfiture of those they manipulate at the same time as they have vicariously insinuated themselves into identical states of betrayal and

[50] An exception to this rule is "A Painful Case." Joyce did not write all the stories in the order he finally arranged them. The composition and publishing history Richard Ellmann has treated in detail in the biography. See also studies by Robert Scholes in *Studies in Bibliography*, volumes 15, 16, and 17, in which he treats textual matters and annotates the correspondence between Grant Richards and Joyce.

frustration. Thus, in the stories, Joyce portrays both "artistic" experience and the response to it. Like Mallarmé's Hamlet, the Dubliners constantly read from the books of themselves, delighting in their own pathos. Book-oriented characters like the adolescents in the first three stories, or Mr. James Duffy in "A Painful Case," or Gabriel in "The Dead," have the added advantage of staging in their own lives the vicarious experience incarnate in print. Surfeited with American detective stories, the lad in "An Encounter" ventures into the "real world" in the hope of achieving the erotic adventure he has read about. He encounters an aged degenerate's pathetic quest for self-humiliation and for the humiliation of others. He travels from one form of staged experience in pulp magazines to another form of staged experience in a lonely meadow.

Throughout *Dubliners*, Joyce demonstrates the power of myth on his compatriots. They cannot free themselves from the recent myths of Ireland, which in *A Portrait* Stephen calls "the nets" of family, nation, religion. Extensions of the dead, these myths are both the media and the rationalizations of sadomasochism. The final effect of sadomasochism is paralysis, the sum total of affective elements in Dublin life. Unlike tribal myths, the governing myths in Dublin appear as fragmented influences in individual lives. But behind the apparent fragmentation a common game of belief pulls the fragments together. For the Dubliners constantly pretend paralysis while their lives actually mask petty power maneuvers. They wear masks they pretend to believe. Occasionally, the mask becomes reality to them: neurosis becomes psychosis. Gradually, the protagonist in "Eveline" convinces herself she *is* her dead mother. Like a savage hypnotic with belief in the mask of god he has been wearing, Eveline goes into a trance to avoid entering the ship which would take her away from Dublin and the need for masks.[51] She

___

[51] Joseph Campbell discusses the relation between belief and illusion in the wearing of the masks of god, common, he explains, not only to the primitives but to all forms of religious ritual. "The Lesson of the Mask" in *The Masks of God: Primitive Mythology* (New York, 1965), pp. 21–29.

becomes entranced with her subtle omnipotence. But she is never so powerless as when convinced of the extent of her power. She identifies with her dead mother as with a tribal god. Her pretense is more apparent to us when her own awareness of pretense has vanished.

More often, the Dubliners are neurotic. Their deceptions constitute a governing mythology. The adoption of masks grows out of the belief that power derives from identification with the dead, who once by a vicious hypnotism ruled Dublin. Father Flynn, of "The Sisters," Gabriel Conroy's mother, in "The Dead," for example, are gods, comprising a homely but effective mythology. They rule through their own masks, worn uneasily by the living. In Joyce's adaptation of Ibsen, these masks are worn by the "living dead." Gabriel's hesitant belief in the omniscience of his dead mother rules from beyond the grave, and therefore he cannot live a creative marriage with Gretta. His continual discomfort testifies to his awareness of the lie. In Joyce's only extant play, *Exiles*, this theme will be carried to its logical extreme and to its most absurd depiction.

Sophisticated and archaic mythologies also serve Dublin's living deceptions. The boy in "Araby" acts the role of chivalry, a parody of medieval play forms, merged with the priestly role of the dead priest who left his relics in an abandoned house the boy frequents.[52] His power the boy pretends by playing the role of chivalric priest, bearing his chalice through a throng of foes. The boy mimics a life he does not feel—either the erotic vivacity of chivalry, or the spiritual life of the liturgy. Courtly love and sacramental devotion show forth as role-playing, devoid of creative play. They neither inspire nor liberate.

Also, in *Dubliners* Joyce parodies the modes of heroism—ro-

[52] "The initiation and dubbing of knights, the enfeoffing of a tenure, tournaments, heraldry, chivalric orders, vows—all these things hark back beyond the classical to a purely archaic past, and in all of them the play factor is powerfully operative and a really creative force." Johan Huizinga, *Homo Ludens* (Boston, 1966), p. 180.

mance, tragedy, comedy—not simply in deference to inevitable forms of literature, but to contrast these heroic modes with the impoverished forms of Dublin. The structure of "Araby," a knightly quest, suggests that it is based on the form of ancient romance. The structure of "A Painful Case," an awareness of despairing death, suggests its basis in tragedy. "The Dead," which recounts Gabriel's second honeymoon, resembles the classic comic structure that traditionally ends with going to bed. In "The Dead," however, the bed is a coffin recalling those apocryphal monastery beds described at the party.

Contemporary criticism perceives modern literature as ironic in the sense I have been describing. Man appears in fiction and on the stage bound to wheels of history, myth, neurosis. Joyce is characteristically modern because at least in his early work he portrays man in such bondage that only a perception of absurdity allows the freedom of laughter. I would not affirm that such is true of all modern literature any more than I would agree that all men are neurotic. However, my procedure ought to demonstrate the extent to which in his early work Joyce was so locked into a perception of the Dubliners as neurotic that he must construct an ironic vision and a series of parodies, right up to *Ulysses*, which is generally regarded as his creation of the uniquely modern form of heroism—discovery of a liberating rather than an enslaving mythos.

The early work of James Joyce depicts neurotic personalities in a neurotic society. The Dubliners are incapable of enjoyment. In "After the Race," Jimmy Doyle shares in the triumph of his foreign friends, but unlike them he cannot be "genuinely happy." The device of vicarious conquest only intensifies his misery. The Dubliners waste their energies. Vivid imaginations and shrewd minds are busy with tipsy alterations of the past, like Maria's brother in "Clay," or with absurd and inaccurate theological discussions as in "Grace." They feel little affection for one another, none at all for outsiders. Even their heroic dead, such as Parnell, in "Ivy Day in the Committee Room," they love within a spirit of backbiting cronyism and

sentimental flatulence. More often, their disposition is one of precise hostility. In the most hospitable of the stories, "The Dead,"
Gabriel acts out a chilling aversion for his wife and for his fellow
Dubliners. In lieu of healthy self-assertion, Joyce's Dubliners usually display neurotic passivity in the face of a debilitating environment, as with the passive adolescent in "The Sisters," and with
Eveline's sadomasochistic helplessness at the end of her story. When
they seem to rebel, like Farrington in "Counterparts," their attacks
are petty and ineffectual, their victories, pyhrric.

In the first two stories, sadomasochism appears in a familiar form,
the vice of old men who would corrupt predisposed adolescents.
Here, sadomasochism operates as in the works of the Divine Marquis, where the supposedly ingenuous succumb to the incorrigibly
corrupt. Early in *Dubliners*, this lurid sadomasochism approaches
pornography and thus may be perceived with relative clarity. But
in the later stories, sadomasochistic neurosis in Dublin takes a
subtler and more pernicious form. The older Dubliners have sur-
rendered to neurosis and have repressed its more exotic manifestations, like Maria in "Clay," under a cover of "demure nods and
hems." As the instinct for sadomasochistic frustration goes underground, the Dublin superego becomes more skillful at disguising it.

In Joyce's Dublin, the adolescent and the senescent are most alive
—the most obviously perverse and therefore the least perverse. By
the time he wrote *Exiles*, he felt obliged to be even more explicit
about the theme of sadomasochism. He said the play was "a rough
and tumble" between de Sade and Sacher-Masoch. Throughout this
study, I demonstrate the way in which this explicit theme in *Exiles*
is implicit in the earlier stories of *Dubliners*. *Ulysses* will embody
Joyce's most sophisticated treatment of this theme.

I have not written on the stories in *Dubliners* in the order Joyce
composed them nor within his own categories of youth, adolescence,
maturity, and public life. I consider the stories as varied exhibitions
of the paralysis at Dublin's center, stressing the solemnity of Dublin
in the first three chapters, but in the fourth the comic side of living

parasitically on the dead, in "Ivy Day in the Committee Room," and the solemn aspect of this in "The Dead." In the fifth chapter, I describe in *Exiles* Joyce's most explicit version of neurosis. Overall, the effect of *Dubliners* and of *Exiles* is, I believe, comic. Since Joyce's problem in *Dubliners* was how to keep a straight face, the style of scrupulous meanness served as a literary deadpan. In *Exiles*, where Joyce deliberately used the pedantic style of Ibsen, he was not able to reconcile his language choice with the lugubrious canvas of Dublin. In any case, by his own admission, an imp guided his pen: "The Dublin papers will object to my stories as to a caricature of Dublin life . . . At times the spirit directing my pen seems to me so plainly mischievous that I am almost prepared to let the Dublin critics have their way."[53]

Because I have not wished to belabor my argument concerning Joyce's depiction of the sadomasochistic neurosis he perceived in Dublin, I do not consider in detail those stories in which this theme is least apparent: "Grace," "The Boarding House," and "A Mother." Nevertheless, the theme is there, if less explicitly than in the other stories. For example, in "The Boarding House," and in "A Mother," apparently helpless men, such as Bob Doran and Hoppy Holohan, employ their passivity to avoid victimization at the hands of domineering women, but at the same time they precipitate their own downfall. Though Joyce looks at his characters with a comic eye, they resemble those tragic figures of nineteenth-century literature, like Hardy's Henchard, of whom Albert Guerard has written: "[they] thrust themselves in the way of bad luck; create what appear to be unlucky accidents."[54] They are victims unconsciously eager; their willingness consistent with Joyce's primarily ironic concept of his stories as "epicleti," or aesthetic invocations by which the artist performs a usually comic transubstantiation of the experience of victimization, and through which the apparently innocent "offer"

[53] Joyce to Stanislaus Joyce, 19 July 1905, *Letters*, vol. 2, p. 99.
[54] Albert Guerard, *Thomas Hardy: The Novels and Stories* (Cambridge, 1949), p. 147.

themselves to the exploitation of power as in the Mass Christ offers Himself to the Father through the priest. Joyce told Stanislaus he thought of his work as similar to that of the priest in the Mass. He was contributing to the spiritual nourishment of his compatriots by changing the bread of everyday circumstance into the eucharist of art.[55] He described *Dubliners* to Constantine Curran as "a series of epicleti," or invocations before the consecration of the Mass.[56] One cannot fail to notice the metaphor in which the everyday victimization of Dublin life becomes an "offering" to the artist-priest, who changes this experience into a form of fiction which ritualistically "celebrates" again and again the experience of sacrifice. By juxtaposition with the Catholic Mass, a "celebration" of Christ's sacrifice, the irony of *Dubliners* appears in clearer form. The sacrifice in Dublin is not really tragic, as was the sacrificial isolation of Christ, because the Dubliners engineer their own victimization and because victimization is on so universal a scale in Dublin that there is no real isolation. In Dublin, every man is crucified on the cross of his own "cruelfiction," to borrow from *Finnegans Wake*.[57] In *Dubliners*, the image of the helpless, paralyzed, ingenuous Dubliner constantly recurs. Less apparent is that, in the absence of real imperium, he cleverly if ineffectually copes with power. His victories are like those of Pyrrhus, whose laconic battle report Cochrane repeats in schoolboy jargon to Stephen in *Ulysses*: "Another victory like that and we are done for" (*Ulysses*, p. 25). Like Pyrrhus, the Dubliner often falls, "by a beldam's hand" (*Ulysses*, p. 26). Unlike Pyrrhus, his hand may guide the hand that undoes him.

Because I hold this view of Joyce's *Dubliners*, I cannot finally agree with the observation that in his early fiction Joyce was a Naturalist. For example, writing about "The Boarding House,"

[55] Stanislaus Joyce, *My Brother's Keeper: James Joyce's Early Years* (New York, 1958), p. 104.

[56] Joyce to Constantine Curran, n.d., 1904, *Letters*, vol. 1, p. 55.

[57] Joyce, *Finnegans Wake* (New York, 1958), p. 192. All subsequent references to *Finnegans Wake* will be from this text. Page references will be in parentheses after the quotation.

W. Y. Tindall maintains that "The Boarding House," "affords comfort to those who think Joyce loyal to Zola. Never was pressure of environment more obviously displayed. Bob Doran's fall, determined by Dublin's moral conventions and hypocrisies, seems exemplary. The theme, like that of any naturalistic story, is this pressure, within which the 'Madam' and her daughter work."[58] However, Doran's "fall" results at least as much from his own not completely naive motivations as from Dublin's moral conventions and hypocrisies. He wants to be seduced into the domestic comfort which his "celibate" inhibitions warn him against. He needs (and wants) a push by the uncompromising mother and daughter. He gets a push in the direction he is willfully aimed. It is an oversimplification to view the story as a vehicle of "pressures of environment," however much these operate directly. To see Joyce as having intended, in the fashion of Zola, to portray "the whole world" conspiring against Doran,[59] is to risk losing sight of Joyce's ironic awareness of the extent of human self-deception: to extirpate Joyce's mischievous sense of comedy. As for Joyce as a naturalist *a la* Zola, he seemed to have found the idea amusing. In regard to *Dubliners* he wrote Grant Richards, "The worst that will happen, I suppose, is that some critic will allude to me as the 'Irish Zola'! But even such a display of the critical intellect should not be sufficiently terrible to deter you from bringing out the book."[60]

[58] W. Y. Tindall, *A Reader's Guide to James Joyce* (New York, 1959), p. 26. Italics mine. Marvin Magalaner solemnly interprets the story in much the same way: he sees Doran as a "creature caught in the web of convention, religious scruples, social tautness, and economic necessity . . . whose intellect counsels flight while an intangible hand holds him fast to all he despises." Magalaner, "James Joyce's *Dubliners*," Ph.D. dissertation (New York, 1951), p. 137. In my view the "intangible hand" is within Doran, not holding him from without. He desires flight, but wants what he flees. Although less simple than that of Magalaner and Tindall, this view seems the only one warranted by the facts.

[59] In his notes for *L'Assommoir*, Zola wrote, "I must show the whole world trying to bring about the ruin [of his heroine, Gervaise] consciously or unconsciously." Matthew Josephson, *Zola and His Time* (New York, 1928), p. 532.

[60] Joyce to Grant Richards, 13 May 1906, *Letters*, vol. 2, p. 137.

In its literary form, sadomasochism is frequently a comic posture. One of Joyce's favorite novels,[61] *Venus in Furs*, the archetype of literary masochism, ends with a smile. Sacher-Masoch's protagonist, Severin, preserves an hysterical decorum throughout his debasement, but the comedy of his perversion breaks through as a sign of health. Observing the cruel Wanda's portrait three years after his final humiliation he says: "I had to smile, and as I fell to musing the beautiful woman suddenly stood before me in her velvet jacket trimmed with ermine, with the whip in her hand. And I continued to smile at the woman I had once loved so insanely, at the fur-jacket that had once so entranced me, at the whip, and ended by smiling at myself and saying: the cure was cruel, but radical; but the main point is, I have been cured."[62] In Joyce's view, the health of Dublin could have proceeded only from his own admittedly malicious laughter.

But we cannot laugh without realizing the serious relevance of his insight for this century, in which complex cruelty has been a central experience. Although not all cruelty is sadomasochistic, all sadomasochism is cruel. Not ever an isolated element in literary works, it provides a whole informing conception and context. We may be distracted by the spectacular behavior in de Sade and Sacher-Masoch, or more recently in *The Painted Bird* and *The Story of O*. We would be imperceptive to dismiss these as aberrations from the current social or literary scene, since this scene is more apt to involve sadomasochism than not. We would be mistaken to regard Joyce's provincial Dublin as little more than a joke of imperial history. He has contributed to the perception of our own extraordinarily complicated time.

Sadomasochism implies so pervasive an attitude towards reality that it permeates the form and content of certain works of art. How-

---

[61] According to Richard Ellmann, Joyce and Nora "shared a jocular affection" for Sacher-Masoch's books. Ellmann, *James Joyce*, pp. 430–431. Ellmann also discusses Joyce's use of *Venus in Furs* in the "Circe" episode of *Ulysses*. *Ibid.*, pp. 380–381.

[62] Leopold von Sacher-Masoch, *Venus in Furs* (New York, 1965), p. 143.

ever, at its most destructive, sadomasochism does not exist in the light of day, just as overt and conscious cruelty will not always be neurotic in the strictest sense of the term. When the neurotic attitude goes underground through the mechanics of repression, it is truly most destructive. The characters in de Sade and in Sacher-Masoch are healthier in the conscious luxury of their quests for pain than the grotesques in Joyce's Dublin. Given appropriate social, economic, political conditions, the demonic efficiency of repressed sadomasochism becomes the pattern of an Eichmann. The banality of petty sadomasochistic meanness becomes what Hannah Arendt has called "the banality of evil." However accurately we perceive the behavior in Joyce's Dublin through his own attitude, we cannot finally rest in a sense of comic detachment.

CHAPTER I

The Green Stem of Fortune:
Paralysis as Prospect

IN THE FIRST THREE STORIES of *Dubliners*, Joyce adumbrates the character of his book as an evaluation of motive. "The Sisters," "An Encounter," "Araby," all portray specific quests by sensitive young Dubliners who stand off from a perverse environment with a degree of disengagement resembling that of Joyce himself. These characters have not yet completely succumbed to the paralysis afflicting their elders, although they envision the possibility of acquiescence. From the start they figure as judges of Dublin because their standards have not yet dissolved in the acid of Dublin's pious immorality. After these three stories and until "The Dead," the reader's judgment depends on its formation by identification with the adolescents in the first three stories; for the stories intervening between the first three and "The Dead" depict protagonists incapable for the most part of detached self-evaluation (with the exceptions of Mr. Duffy in "A Painful Case" and Little Chandler in "A Little Cloud," both of whom light up their lives long enough to see the wreckage, but not long enough to escape). Even Gabriel acquiesces in the annihilating snow that covers Dublin, and we perceive him through the eyes of the first three protagonists.

Upon the death of a paralytic priest who had taught and befriended him, the boy in "The Sisters" discovers that earlier the priest had broken down after having inadvertently broken a chalice.

35

Through his acquaintance with the priest and through what he discovers about him posthumously the boy achieves a kind of realization—the goal to which the whole work tends. His realization differs from the climax of the story, in fact, stems from it. The chief irritant is the boy's conflict with the adult world because of his relationship with the priest, disapproved of by Old Cotter, for example, who knows something about the priest of which the boy appears ignorant. In the end the boy's apparent ignorance disappears and his epiphany occurs.

Joyce foreshadows the discovery when coming downstairs for supper, the boy hears Old Cotter say, "—No, I wouldn't say he was exactly . . . but there was something queer . . . something uncanny about him. I'll tell you my opinion" (pp. 9–10). Although angry with Old Cotter ("Tiresome old red-nosed imbecile!" p. 11), the boy puzzles to "extract meaning from his unfinished sentences" (p. 11). Following this presentation of the problem, is an account of the boy's relation with the priest, his initial uneasiness about the priest, and finally his visit to the house where the priest lay in his coffin. Here Eliza provides some explanation of Old Cotter's earlier remarks when she recalls that the old priest had broken a chalice, and had been discovered later in his confessional "wide-awake and laughing-like softly to himself" (p. 18).

Structurally, the problem in the story occurs as a question presented about the old priest. The question intensifies through the retelling of the boy's relationship to the priest, and his reactions to this relationship. Finally, it is answered with an account of the priest's breakdown and its immediate cause. The resolution comes with the boy's winning a partial solution to his initial puzzle from those of the adult world who know the priest's secret. In this sense he is a protagonist, although his struggle for an answer is wholly interior, and even deliberately hidden from his adult antagonists: "Old Cotter looked at me for a while. I felt that his little beady black eyes were examining me but I would not satisfy him by looking up from my plate" (p. 10). Furthermore, the boy is aware of his own fear of finding out the truth he seeks: "I wished to go in and look at him but I had not the courage to knock" (p. 12).

From this simple structure Joyce derives a complicated psychic movement, some of it carefully veiled within his protagonist and within the warped disposition of the priest. He has also prepared the ground for fourteen other stories and planted seeds of meaning and technique which may be seen in *A Portrait of the Artist as a Young Man,* and which will flower in *Ulysses* and *Finnegans Wake.*

A formulation of the object of the boy's quest, the final internal goal of the story, obliges the reader to look with the protagonist at the spiritual condition of the priest, through an evaluation of which the protagonist's epiphany comes about. The boy appears to desire to be a free person in his own right; his compulsive relation with the neurotic priest has enslaved and inhibited him. The priest certainly represents corrupt features of Irish Catholicism, so it goes without saying that Joyce is making a more universal comment on the servile relation of the Dubliners to ecclesiastical authority.[1] But the task here is to determine the boy's quest for a specific benefit and the relation of this quest to his personal involvement with the priest.

The boy appears to want to be free to achieve the fulfilling joy without which one cannot live satisfactorily, and his relationship with the priest is an obstacle. When the priest dies the boy discovers "that neither I nor the day seemed in a mourning mood and I felt even annoyed at discovering in myself a sensation of freedom as if I had been freed from something by his death. I wondered at this . . ." (p. 12). After reading the funeral notice he feels a "sensation of freedom" which any sensitive youth might prefer instead of an oppressive relationship with a decaying old man. Still the boy in some way wants that relationship. He feels "annoyed" at discovering in himself a sensation of freedom, just as earlier he had been

---

[1] For Marvin Magalaner, Joyce illustrates in the dying priest the "decaying Irish Catholic God." *Joyce: The Man, the Work, the Reputation* (New York, 1962), p. 84.

angered at Old Cotter who disapproved of his relationship with the priest on the grounds that it was "bad for children" (p. 10). Although the reader is obviously expected to shudder at the priest and what he represents, there is no question of the boy's attraction for what at the same time he abhors—the infectious corruption of a degenerate old man. The first paragraph of the story ends with the well-known statement that "[*paralysis*] sounded to me like the name of some maleficent and sinful being. It filled me with fear, and yet I longed to be nearer to it and to look upon its deadly work" (p. 9). The boy is drawn to a contemplation of what, infecting him, would inhibit his freedom. One clue to his attraction appears in his phantasm the night after his discovery of the priest's death: "In the dark of my room I imagined that I saw again the heavy grey face of the paralytic. I drew the blankets over my head and tried to think of Christmas. But the grey face still followed me. It murmured; and I understood that it desired to confess something. I felt my soul receding into some *pleasant and vicious* region; and there again I found it waiting for me" (p. 11, italics mine).

Revolted by the perverse face, the boy tries to dispel the image, with thoughts of Christmas, which would promise a redemption from compulsions; but this tactic fails, and the boy retreats still further into a region where although the pleasure is not clearly specified it is nonetheless attractively vicious. Here again the grey image waits, and the boy stops where he finds himself cornered by his compulsive, fearful, but still pleasantly corrupt relation with the priest. It is as though the decaying priest were trying to bequeath his own sacerdotal corruption, to which the boy has become so addicted that to be freed from it (even though he tries to retreat) would require too painful a withdrawal. At the end of the phantasm the roles are reversed: the boy is now a confessor, smiling with the vague perversity of his mentor: "[The face] began to confess to me in a murmuring voice and I wondered why it smiled continually and why the lips were so moist with spittle. But then I remembered that it had died of paralysis and I felt that I too was smiling feebly as if to absolve the simoniac of his sin" (p. 11).

The boy's compulsive devotion to a vicious quest forces him to assume the "act" of alienated observer: his stance is the necessary corollary to his divided nature. On the one hand he appears however weakly to display the usual adolescent enthusiasm. He walks on the sunny side of the street looking at the theatrical advertisements on a day of mourning. On the way to the wake he notices that "the window-panes of the houses that looked to the west reflected the tawny gold of a great bank of clouds" (p. 14). But his devotion to the old priest forces him to behave towards other adults with a sanctimonious calm which belies his true feelings: when Old Cotter objects to his relation with the priest, the boy crams his mouth with cereal "for fear I might give utterance to . . . anger" (p. 11). And later, at the wake, the boy puts on an air of piety the reverse of his true feelings.

The boy's refusal of the biscuits and his initial refusal of sherry at the wake have been interpreted cleverly, but I think not accurately, as a refusal to partake of the sacraments, as his rejection of the Church.[2] However, in context, the boy actually rejects the secular sacraments of the women who assume a priestly role, because, even though the priest is dead, the boy still savors the wine of the perverse sacraments they had celebrated together. He is not rejecting the Church, for in context this would be to achieve a joyful freedom. He is rejecting conventional experience, proferred to him by well-meaning old women who cannot provide him with a surrogate for the pleasant and vicious region where in imagination he lives with the old priest. The gesture of refusal is at the same time a gesture of allegiance.

The boy's devotion to a perverse relationship with the priest becomes clearer on investigation of the priest's character and his relationship with the boy. Clearly the priest's paralysis, resulting from

[2] *Ibid.*, pp. 85–86.

hemiplegic stroke, images his spiritual condition and, by synecdoche, that of Dublin in general, which Joyce referred to as "hemiplegia."[3] The disease follows an act which the priest interprets as
a spiritual transgression. He had broken a chalice, which mishap
"affected his mind" (p. 17) to the extent that shortly afterwards he
had been discovered in the confessional-box "wide-awake and
laughing-like softly to himself" (p. 19). The only direct explanation
for the priest's behavior is Eliza's assertion that "poor James was
so nervous. . . ." (p. 17). She also says that "—He was too scrupulous
always . . . The duties of the priesthood was too much for him. And
then his life was, you might say, crossed" (p. 17). The apparently
inadvertent mishandling of an empty chalice could not itself have
accounted for the priest's breakdown, but no cause beyond this act
is directly given in the story and the only explanation of the act
itself is that he was "nervous." The remote causes of the priest's
"nervousness" are hidden behind Eliza's mysterious assertion that
his life had been "crossed," and the no less enigmatic seconding of
Nannie, "—Yes . . . He was a disappointed man. You could see that"
(p. 17). Joyce has left the reader to conjecture from various hints
the priest's unfortunate background, and a substantial conjecture
is needed to explain the priest's mysterious hold on the protagonist.

One imagines that the priest finds in the boy compensation for a
quest in which he had been mysteriously "disappointed," that thing
unnamed in which he had been "crossed," frustrated in some strong
desire. Because of this lack of fulfillment "the duties of the priesthood was too much for him." The boy thinks early in the story of
the word "gnomon" in connection with "paralysis" with its obvious
meaning, and "simony" with its somewhat less obvious meaning
in context. Like most of the Dubliners, the priest is a "gnomon";
he has not fulfilled himself as a person which means exactly that he
has not achieved union with that unique benefit which would have

[3] Joyce to Constantine P. Curran, n.d., 1904, *Letters*, vol. 1, ed. Stuart Gilbert
(New York, 1966), p. 55.

precluded the necessity for speaking of him as "disappointed."[4] His relationship with the boy is a deflected quest for him, a surrogate for true fulfillment.

The breaking of a chalice represents the penultimate stage in a dissolution of priestly commitment which relieves the priest of a species of unfulfilling behavior. His breakdown in the confessional signals the final breaking of commitment. Afterwards a series of "strokes" gradually destroys his commitment to life itself and in his last days he is free to devote himself to a quasi-spiritual liaison with a sensitive boy. This relationship allows his frustrated desires to play out their last chance for fulfillment, only now in a soul-destroying way. The priestly role clearly did not suffice as a surrogate for disappointed expectation. The priest was obliged to slough off a role which was "too much for him" because it did not satisfy his quest. His later relationship with the boy substituted for what the priestly role had failed to satisfy.

There is about this peculiar relationship an odor of perversity because in his role as spiritual father and teacher the priest seduces the boy away from the enthusiasms of childhood into an attachment to the pleasantly vicious sweets of spiritual seduction in which there is apparently an element of erotic perversity, which is never overt. Though he was asked about it, Joyce was not explicit on this point. He wrote Stanislaus, "Roberts I saw again. He asked me very narrowly was there sodomy also in *The Sisters* as in "An Encounter" and what was 'simony' and if the priest was suspended only for the breaking of the chalice."[5] Joyce does not answer the question, even in his letter to Stanislaus. But there is a hint at perversity in the

---

[4] A "gnomon" in geometry is a parallelogram with one corner removed: a figure with something missing. Gerhard Friedrich has pointed out the importance of "gnomon" as a sign for the general spiritual condition of Joyce's Dubliners. "The Gnomonic Clue to James Joyce's *Dubliners*," *MLN* 72 (June 1957): 421–424.

[5] Joyce to Stanislaus Joyce, 20 August 1912, *Letters*, vol. 2, ed. Richard Ellman (New York, 1966), pp. 305–306.

boy's struggle to recall what came in the dream after his absolution of the priest: "I remembered that I had noticed long velvet curtains and a swinging lamp of antique fashion. I felt that I had been very far away, in some land where the customs were strange—in Persia, I thought. . . . But I could not remember the end of the dream" (pp. 13–14). There is also a hint of perversity in the description of the priest smiling: "he used to uncover his big discoloured teeth and let his tongue lie upon his lower lip— a habit which had made me feel uneasy in the beginning of our acquaintance before I knew him well" (p. 13). Finally, the title, "The Sisters," refers not only to Nannie and Eliza, but to an effeminate relationship between the priest and his disciple.

There is little evidence that Joyce wants them to be thought of as engaging in overt sexuality. The physical disability of the priest and the social context probably preclude such an affair. More clear is the priest's sadistic posture, the boy's masochism. The priest derives pleasure from a relationship in which he can inflict the double pain of his revolting presence and his Jansenistic doctrine, for both of these exercise on the boy so mysteriously strong an attraction that he feels compelled to look on the loathsome work of physical and spiritual paralysis in spite of (or perhaps because of) his great fear. The boy feels attracted to the priest *because of* the pain he derives from the relationship. The pain stems from his desire to be paralyzed in the way of the priest—especially to be so tied up spiritually that determined action would be hindered by a legal system literally impossible to understand because of its infinitely casuistic character: "Sometimes he had amused himself by putting difficult questions to me, asking me what one should do in certain circumstances or whether such and such sins were mortal or venial or only imperfections. His questions showed me how complex and mysterious were certain institutions of the Church which I had always regarded as the simplest acts (p. 13)." The boy discovers "the simplest acts" so complex that action is either impossible or fraught with terrible implications. This belief concerning action, linked as it is with the authority of the Church, is a statement of the spiritual paralysis which has destroyed the priest as a human and which, working on the boy, is likely to bring him to the same pass. The priest "had amused himself" in the act of infecting the boy with a paralytic doctrine, for apparently his relationship with the boy was a surrogate by which he could now get pleasure; and the boy falls victim to the pleasure of being seduced into a state of paralyzed passivity, that pleasant and vicious area in his soul.

In his natural quest for fulfillment through pleasurable activity the boy finds his quest converted into pleasure through painful inability to act. The realization and the prospect of the priest's paralysis appeal to the boy more strongly than the prospect of living warmth represented by "the tawny gold of a great bank of clouds," wistfully glimpsed on the way to the wake.

The boy seeks the characteristically human activities of knowledge and friendship; his relationship with the priest corrupts both activities and dehumanizes him. Gradually his quest for knowledge has been frustrated by the priest's corruption of his reason, for the priest's lessons infect his student with a paralyzing scepticism. The priest's disquisitions are neither speculative nor scientific but practical. His questioning and his teaching are apparently taken up entirely with moral theology, which pertains to modes of action. But the boy tastes an even more bitter fruit in the corruption of his hunger for the activity of friendship—the paralysis of his capacity for human relationships about which he has a significant revelation. He dimly realizes that the priest had used him for his own surrogate gains, for his own neurotic pleasure. Furthermore the boy realizes that he had used the priest for the same thing. They had used each other as substitute persons for unsatisfactory personal relations in the past, which is why in his phantasm the boy smiles feebly "as though to absolve the simoniac of his sin."[6] The priest had "sold"

[6] Julian B. Kaye discusses the theme of simony in *Dubliners* in "Simony, the Three Simons, and Joycean Myth" in *A James Joyce Miscellany*, ed. Marvin Magalaner (New York, 1957), pp. 20–36.

his "spiritual gifts," in context, his priestly knowledge and his sacramental role for the perverse gain of hypnotic seduction. The boy
"absolves" him because the seduction has filled his own personal
need. The feeble smile, like that of the priest, is a smile of mutual
understanding, mutual acquiescence, and mutual pleasure in a
sadomasochistic system in which both persons get what they need,
as is invariably the case in that series of sadomasochistic liaisons
throughout *Dubliners*. A moral purpose of Joyce's writing is to
free his compatriots (and perhaps himself) from their enslavement
to sadomasochism. Thus, he wrote Grant Richards: "I believe that
in composing my chapter of moral history in exactly the way I have
composed it I have taken the first step towards the spiritual liberation of my country."[7]

The boy's quest for pleasure in a sadomasochistic relationship is
a deflection of his search for freedom, for self-fulfillment, for the
joy of life. He seeks both the relationship itself and, because he is
troubled, he seeks an awareness about the nature of the relationship.
Part of this is a wistful awareness of the *joie de vivre* which the
surrogate replaces. Joyce expresses the boy's complex desire through
a series of images which the critic must illuminate and from which
he must isolate a concept of the protagonist's quest. Joyce's method
is to present those images conveying the underlying quest in a
juxtaposition which suggests his evaluation. With its repulsive
associations "the heavy grey face of the paralytic" haunts "The
Sisters." It is the most fearful and enticing image of quest. The boy
can find untroubled satisfaction in relatively few images and these
never enchant him for long. During his bedtime phantasm he tries
without success to shun the image of the gargoyle face by thinking
of Christmas. His walk on the sunny side of the street looking at
"theatrical advertisements," implying a life away from nightmare
reality, and his later reflected vision of golden clouds are intermit-
tent images. The images weigh towards the compulsively perverse
and against the naturally attractive, which suggests the relative

[7] Joyce to Grant Richards, 20 May 1906, *Letters*, vol. 1, pp. 62–63.

weight of perverse and normal motivation in "The Sisters." The reader's epiphany comes as he assesses the image force in the story. At the end when Eliza comments, "so then, of course, when they saw that, that made them think that there was something gone wrong with him," the reader perceives that the deflected quest is the main thing wrong with Dublin. Along with Joyce, we evaluate Dublin life. Carefully, we peer into Joyce's mirror and "think that there was something gone wrong."

The structure of "An Encounter" is quite simple. Oppressed by everyday school routine, a young boy, with his adventurous companion, plays truant to undertake an expedition to the "Pigeon House" (Dublin's powerhouse). At first exuberant, the boys become subdued when time and fatigue prevent them from reaching their goal, and in this mood they encounter an older man who, from his words and actions, is shown to be perverse. The boys escape from their unpleasant encounter and return home.

The tension-creating stimulus in "An Encounter" is the restrictive school environment of the boy. His tendency towards satisfaction of a youthful urge is hemmed in by a stern authority figure who insists on recitations about imperial Rome, the authority symbol in the story contrasted with the barbaric west: "One day when Father Butler was hearing the four pages of Roman History clumsy Leo Dillon was discovered with a copy of *The Halfpenny Marvel*. . . . —What is this rubbish? he said. *The Apache Chief*! Is this what you read instead of studying your Roman History?" (p. 20). The lines are early drawn between stern patriarchal authority and youthful barbarism, although the protagonist's urge to get away from authority takes a more erotic form than that of his schoolmates with their cowboys and Indians play. "The adventures related in the literature of the Wild West were remote from my nature but, at least, they opened doors of escape. I liked better some American detective stories which were traversed from time to time by unkempt fierce and beautiful girls" (p. 20). Consequently, the protagonist's quest, in part originating in erotic tension, takes the inchoate form of a thirst for "wild sensations" which he expects to achieve through falling upon "real adventures."

W. Y. Tindall concentrates on the story as a quest for "the Pigeon House," which he interprets (following Magalaner's insight) as the "traditional icon for the Holy Ghost." He goes on to say that "the quest . . . can be taken as a search for the third member of the Trinity or, since Father, Son and Holy Ghost are one, as that hunt for a father which was to become a theme of *Ulysses*."[8] Tindall's interpretation does not explain why the boy desires experiences at the hands of "wild women." It is not altogether certain that Joyce meant the "Pigeon House" as a symbol. However, if symbolic, the Pigeon House would seem to symbolize women, since the boy seeks a passive relation with women; he seeks seduction, therefore a kind of erotic domination. The Pigeon House is Dublin's powerhouse, and in Dublin the women more often than not wield power (as in "A Mother," "The Boarding House," etc.). At the same time, the boy flees from women, if we identify him with the pervert he sees potentially in himself. He does not seek a father ultimately, but proximately as an authority figure and, through perversion, as a substitute for the wild women who are the ultimate but, for him, unattainable objects of his search.

The resolution is in the boy's encounter with the pervert. The erotic tension generated earlier subsides, so that just before the old man's appearance, the movement in the story seems practically to have ceased: "It was too late and we were too tired to carry out our project of visiting the Pigeon House. . . . The sun went in behind some clouds and left us to our jaded thoughts and the crumbs of our provisions" (p. 24). Not perceiving the organic unity of the story, Stanislaus Joyce felt it broke in half at this point: "What is the meaning of writing one half of a story about 'Joe and Leo Dillon' and the other half about a sodomite?"[9] He did not see that his brother had rendered a complicated insight about Dublin's habitual

---

[8] W. Y. Tindall, *A Reader's Guide to James Joyce* (New York, 1959), p. 17.
[9] Stanislaus Joyce to Joyce, 10 October 1905, *Letters*, vol. 2, p. 115.

deflection of erotic quest into surrogate forms. For here in "An Encounter" the old man appears while the protagonist lazily watches, chewing "one of those green stems on which girls tell fortunes" (p. 24), thus, reinforcing the notion that the boy comes to envision himself in a feminine sexual role. The "green" stem connects with the connotations of "green" throughout the story. Related to the boy's quest for erotic adventure is his search for "green eyed sailors," of whom he had a "confused notion." The pervert wears a suit of "greenish-black," by which Marvin Magalaner has associated him with the priest in "The Sisters."[10] The climactic episode in "An Encounter" comes when the boy "involuntarily"—through masochistic compulsion—glances at the old man's face and meets "the gaze of a pair of bottle-green eyes peering . . . from under a twitching forehead" (p. 27).

From here on the disposition for masochistic oppression which the boy had tried to escape by playing truant, the tendency which had appeared in his kow-towing to peers (he was one of the "reluctant Indians who were afraid to seem studious or lacking in robustness," p. 20) reappears. It compels him into a hypnotic submission to the old man's discourse. He breaks away only by main force: "I stood up abruptly. Lest I should betray my agitation I delayed a few moments pretending to fix my shoe properly and then, saying that I was obliged to go, I bade him good-day" (pp. 27–28).

In between his initial urge for masochistic oppression and his abrupt breaking away from the old pervert, the protagonist experiences gradual initiation into the sadomasochism which is the specific form his quest takes, once the opportunity has presented itself at a hiatus in what would appear to be conventional adolescent erotic wish-fulfillment. The boy envisions what might become of him in Dublin, his vision a forecast of the sadomasochism which will permeate the rest of the stories, and Joyce's other works as well. Joyce will, for example, describe the dramatic action in *Exiles* as

[10] Magalaner, *Joyce*, p. 87.

a rough and tumble between the Marquis de Sade and Leopold von Sacher-Masoch.[11] However, the prophecy is not just projected but realized in this story. The boy has in him the itch of masochism; his encounter with the pervert makes actual a tendency which has appeared in him from the beginning of the story when he had subjected himself to the pressures of his peers contrary to his naturally more studious and somewhat less juvenile inclinations, and when, like the typical Joycean male, he had wanted adventures to "happen" to him, rather than to initiate them.[12]

The initiation rite, from which the nonmasochistic Mahoney escapes to active pursuits, draws the protagonist further into a sadomasochistic system into which he wishes to be drawn. After inquiring whether the boys had sweethearts, and being told that Mahoney had "three" and the protagonist none, the man's discourse fades into hypnotic incantation:

> He began to speak to us about girls, saying what nice soft hair they had and how soft their hands were and how all girls were not so good as they seemed to be if only one knew. There was nothing he liked, he said, so much as looking at a nice young girl, at her nice white hands and her beautiful soft hair. He gave me the impression that he was repeating something which he had learned by heart or that, magnetized by some words of his own speech, his mind was slowly circling round and round in the same orbit. At times he spoke as if he were simply alluding to some fact that everybody knew, and at times he lowered his voice and spoke mysteriously as if he were telling us something secret which he did not wish others to overhear. He repeated his phrases over and over again, varying them and surrounding them with his monotonous voice. I continued to gaze towards the foot of the slope, listening to him. (p. 26)

After his initial incantation, the old man goes off and performs a perverse gesture and then returns. His monologue revolves in a new and more explicitly sadomasochistic orbit:

[11] Joyce's notes to *Exiles* (New York, 1965), p. 124.

[12] One recalls that in *A Portrait of the Artist* Stephen could not take the first step in his encounter with a prostitute but had to *be* seduced by her.

He said that if he ever found a boy talking to girls or having a girl
for a sweetheart he would whip him and whip him; and that would
teach him not to be talking to girls. And if a boy had a girl for a
sweetheart and told lies about it then he would give him such a
whipping as no boy ever got in this world. He said that there was
nothing in this world he would like so well as that. He described to
me how he would whip such a boy as if he were unfolding some
elaborate mystery. He would love that, he said, better than anything
in this world; and his voice, as he led me monotonously through the
mystery, grew almost affectionate and seemed to plead with me that
I should understand him. (p. 27)

Like the boy in "The Sisters," the protagonist in "An Encounter"
is lured by the mystery of initiation into a sadomasochistic system
with a degenerate old man. The evocation of a "state" in which he
can find a kind of satisfaction appeals to him. That he does at the
end of the story break away and turn with relief to the nonmasochistic Mahoney suggests Joyce's evaluation: "My voice had an accent
of forced bravery in it and I was ashamed of my paltry stratagem.
I had to call the name again before Mahoney saw me and hallooed
in answer. How my heart beat as he came running across the field
to me! He ran as if to bring me aid. And I was penitent; for in my
heart I had always despised him a little" (p. 28).

From the harsher portrayals of Dublin's youth encountering perversity in the first two stories, Joyce turns to romance. For "Araby"
displays characteristics of "Romance" described by Northrop Frye
in *Anatomy of Criticism* most clearly as it concerns the hero's
power of action: "If superior in *degree* to other men and to his environment, the hero is the typical hero of romance, whose actions
are marvelous but who is himself identified as a human being. The
hero of romance moves in a world in which the ordinary laws of
nature are slightly suspended."[13] Although like all the stories in
Dubliners, "Araby" falls most obviously into the ironic mode, for
the reader finds himself "looking down on a scene of bondage, frus-

[13] Northrop Frye, *Anatomy of Criticism* (Princeton, 1957), p. 33.

tration, or absurdity,"[14] the protagonist attempts to transcend his limitations by "romantic" means. He earnestly imagines a "eucharistic" suspension of the laws of nature. Of course, Joyce works most effectively by mingling the ironic and romantic modes, as he will mix the tragic and ironic in "A Painful Case," the comic and ironic in "The Dead." In all three stories the "heroism" cannot be purely romantic, tragic, or comic because of the sadomasochistic motivations at work. These motivations undermine the archetypal "purity" of romantic, tragic, comic quests. For example, the romantic quest of the boy in "Araby" proves a delusion because the boy realizes his contempt for the romantic gratification he appears to want. He prefers frustration, though he wears the trappings of desire. In "A Painful Case," Mr. Duffy cannot evoke an unequivocal pity because compulsively he engineers his own tragic isolation. In "The Dead," Gabriel cannot be a "pure" comic hero because his desire for the comic bride, Gretta, is undercut by an inhibiting hatred for her. The "irony" of Dubliners is not in showing up how foolish these characters are for thinking they can pretend heroism in Dublin. Rather, it is in showing the reader's archetypal expectations as delusions. They will not bear up under the sharp gaze of Joyce, whose eyes are ours for the duration of our reading. A close look at "Araby" will reveal this special Joycean irony.

In "Araby" an adolescent boy is romantically attracted to a neighbor girl, although he does not communicate with her until in a casual meeting she asks him if he is going to a bazaar called "Araby"; he attends the bazaar to buy a gift for the girl but, delayed by his uncle, he arrives as it is closing and buys nothing.

The protagonist's goal appears to be the indirect manifestation of his feelings to the girl; he goes to "Araby" like a troubadour-knight in the service of his lady.[15] He is inhibited from expressing

[14] *Ibid.*, p. 34.
[15] Cleanth Brooks observed the symbolic character of the boy's actions: "The present he hopes to bring her from Araby would somehow serve as a means of communicating his feelings to her, a symbol for their relationship in the

himself directly to her; like Chaucer's courtly Troilus he watches her from afar: "Every morning I lay on the floor in the front parlour watching her door. The blind was pulled down to within an inch of the sash so that I could not be seen" (p. 30). But his quest is more elaborate than a juvenile attempt to give a shy valentine. One must look at the sacramental element in the story to delineate this intricate quest.

The protagonist actually seeks union not with the girl directly but with her image, a surrogate both for the religious belief which he has virtually given up as dead and hopeless and for an actual relationship with a girl which is also so hopeless for him that he cannot bring himself even to consider it openly. The defining circumstances of his quest suggest both what it replaces and what its character as surrogate must be. The story begins with the description of North Richmond Street which, by synecdoche for all the ways of Dublin, is a dead-end street at the "blind end" of which stands an uninhabited house where a priest had died leaving behind the "old useless papers" of his career. Among these are Scott's *The Abbot*, *The Devout Communicant*, and *The Memoirs of Vidocq*, which in their uselessness evoke both the ineffectuality of religion and the futility of romance in Dublin. The futility of religion has been explored especially in "The Sisters," as in this story the death of romance, but it is romance in a "sacramental" sense, even though the chivalric trappings are present. The youthful crusader's first encounter with his "lady" suggests the ritual of a courtly *donnoi*:

> She asked me was I going to *Araby* . . . . While she spoke she turned a silver bracelet round and round her wrist. She could not go, she said, because there would be a retreat that week in her convent. Her brother and two other boys were fighting for their caps and I was alone at the railings. She held one of the spikes, bowing her head towards me. The light from the lamp opposite our door caught the white curve of her neck, lit up her hair that rested there and, falling,

midst of the inimical world." Brooks and Robert Penn Warren, *Understanding Fiction* (New York, 1959), p. 190.

> lit up the hand upon the railing. It fell over one side of her dress and caught the white border of her petticoat, just visible as she stood at ease. (pp. 31–32)

The erotic implication of the bracelet and the spike is unmistakable, as is the suggestion of her acquiescence in his desire for her. But his quest is not simply erotic, nor even simply at the level of romantic transcendence. His quest for her is combined with his quest for a priestly role. Here, as in the courtly love tradition, religion and romance combine with the difference of course that the medieval system employed religious elements as a convention largely because they were readily available. But in this story and throughout Joyce's writing, religious elements, particularly the liturgical and sacramental, unite with romance in an order not primarily romantic or religious, but a new combination: the transubstantiation of experience which "Araby" describes.

This "sacramental" process can be shown in "Araby" by assuming from the start the boy's identification with the dead priest, in terms of which he carries out his peculiar and isolated adventure. If the story chiefly depicted shy adolescent love, overwrought and disappointed, one could not account for the attention given to these squalid relics of a dead priest. But the first two paragraphs focus on his abandoned house which is a parody of the ruined monastery essential to gothic tales, haunted by sacred ghosts. Joyce's Dublin is one of the first cities to be haunted by modern ghosts— wasteland figures from a past which was neither vital or romantic, living in houses with pretentious histories, like "the house on Usher's Island" in "The Dead"; or Mr. Duffy's parody of a hermitage in "A Painful Case." In Dublin, imagination must have its reliquaries, even at the cost of parody. The shy and curious protagonist had poked about in this house enough to describe with affection the objects left behind. He reveres especially the old "useless" books: "I liked the last [*The Memoirs of Vidocq*] best because its leaves were yellow" (p. 29). After these introductory descriptions, the story recounts the boy's infatuation with Mangan's sister, who, like the priest, affects him entirely from a distance: "I did not know whether I would ever speak to her or not or, if I spoke to her, how I could tell her of my confused adoration. But my body was like a harp and her words and gestures were like fingers running upon the wires" (p. 31).

The tension built up by his "confused adoration" comes to a head when the boy goes into the room where the priest had died: "It was a dark rainy evening and there was no sound in the house. Through one of the broken panes I heard the rain impinge upon the earth, the fine incessant needles of water playing in the sodden beds. Some distant lamp or lighted window gleamed below me. I was thankful that I could see so little. All my senses seemed to desire to veil themselves and, feeling that I was about to slip from them, I pressed the palms of my hands together until they trembled, murmuring: *O love! O love!* many times" (p. 31). Just before this episode, the boy had described himself in a priestly role, listening to "the shrill litanies of shop-boys . . . the nasal chanting of street-singers," sounds which "converged in a single sensation of life for me: I imagined that I bore my chalice safely through a throng of foes. Her name sprang to my lips at moments in strange prayers and praises which I myself did not understand" (p. 31).

Priest-like, the boy carries his eucharist, the image of Mangan's sister. The intense incident in the priest's room implies the verging on a suprasensory transcendence of the conditions of reality. The climax of tension in his rubbing of his hands together is also an invocation, his murmuring "*O love! O love!* many times." Probably also it is an autoerotic displacement. The boy does carry out his erotic desire for Mangan's sister in fantasy which includes eros and eucharist, though the girl is not thought of primarily with affection but with veneration. The sexual element appears mainly through symbolic suggestion, as she turns a bracelet idly on her wrist and holds a fence spike while bowing in assent towards him, like Polly in "The Boarding House," an obscene madonna.[16] The masochistic aspect of this posture Joyce recognized in his own affairs. In a letter to Nora he desired flagellation along with the visual realization of her in the typical Joycean image of woman as an obscene madonna: "Tonight I have an idea madder than usual. I feel I would like to be flogged by you. I would like to see your eyes blazing with anger. I wonder is there some madness in me. Or is love madness? One moment I see you like a virgin or madonna the next moment I see you shameless, insolent, half-naked and obscene."[17]

In "Araby," the moment of invocation leads at once to a description of the first actual encounter between the protagonist and Mangan's sister, with his promise to bring her something from "Araby." After this, "the syllables of the word *Araby* were called to me through the silence in which my soul luxuriated and cast an Eastern enchantment over me" (p. 32). An "Eastern enchantment" urges the boy once again into a posture of transcendence. On the night he goes to "Araby" the ticking clock annoyingly reminds him of the conditions of reality, from which he wishes to flee into his interior state of sacramental transcendence:

> I mounted the staircase and gained the upper part of the house. The high cold empty gloomy rooms liberated me and I went from room to room singing. From the front window I saw my companions playing below in the street. Their cries reached me weakened and indistinct and, leaning my forehead against the cool glass, I looked over at the dark house where she lived. I may have stood there for an hour, seeing nothing but the brown-clad figure cast by my imagination, touched discreetly by the lamplight at the curved neck, at the hand upon the railings and at the border below the dress. (p. 33)

Adequately to achieve his quest, the boy must escape the vivacious sounds and warmth of life, where the clock speaks of human limita-

[16] Mr. Harry Stone presents a long list of archetypal and literary elements in this story, among them the liaison of harlot and "Lady of Romance," as a "pose" on the part of Mangan's sister. " 'Araby' and the Writings of James Joyce," *The Antioch Review* 25 (Fall, 1965): 375–410.

[17] Joyce to Nora, September 2, 1909, *Letters*, vol. 2, p. 243.

tion into a state where passion freezes through the operation of the intellect and imagination: "leaning my forehead against the cool glass, I looked over at the dark house where she lived."[18] As with Stephen Dedalus, in his relation with Emma at the end of *A Portrait*, here at work is "the spiritual—heroic refrigerating apparatus, invented and patented in all countries by Dante Alighieri" (*Portrait*, p. 252).

The story ends with his coming to "Araby," a rapidly darkening hall where it appears that he is not so much disillusioned about the sham nature of his quest as about his desire for what the surrogate replaced. Both encounters with women in the story occur across symbolic barriers and the last, with the salesgirl, conduces to the epiphany. She is the terminus of the protagonist's quest from whom he will presumably buy a trinket to manifest his romantic feelings. But when he arrives at "Araby" she is talking with two young Englishmen. The protagonist finds himself at once in a traditionally inferior position with respect to the salesgirl, who is surrounded by objects symbolically erotic: "Observing me the young lady came over and asked me did I wish to buy anything. The tone of her voice was not encouraging; she seemed to have spoken to me out of a sense of duty. I looked humbly at the great jars that stood like eastern guards at either side of the dark entrance to the stall and murmured: —No, thank you" (p. 35). His turning away implies the rejection of an erotic commitment felt to be futile at least partially because of that feeling of sexual inadequacy typical of the Joycean male. The dominating English command her attention, and the protagonist achieves an epiphany

---

[18] Denis Donoghue perceives a similar pattern in everything Joyce wrote: "Joyce's career is an instance . . . of the gradual abandonment of the finite order, the virtual rejection of the human, the dissolution of time and history." "Joyce and the Finite Order," *Sewanee Review* 68 (Spring, 1960): 270. Though an unqualified generalization about Joyce's work, it suggests something which Joyce criticizes in his compatriots, who invariably prefer to rise above the conditions of existence, the world of "fact," into the ornate realm of Irish imagination.

constituted partially of his feeling of ultimate rejection by the woman and partially of awareness of his own crushed masculinity. "I lingered before her stall, though I knew my stay was useless, to make my interest in her wares seem the more real. Then I turned away slowly and walked down the middle of the bazaar. I allowed the two pennies to fall against the sixpence in my pocket. I heard a voice call from one end of the gallery that the light was out. The upper part of the hall was now completely dark" (p. 35). Once again, the principle of defeat in his quest resides in a pleasant and vicious area of the soul. The itch of masochism urges him finally to look into the sad darkness of self-awareness: "Gazing up into the darkness I saw myself as a creature driven and derided by vanity; and my eyes burned with anguish and anger" (p. 35).

Like most of the Dubliners, the protagonist in "Araby" turns back on the threshold of what he has apparently sought. Like Eveline, who refuses erotic possibilities at the barrier of "the black mass of the ship"; like Mr. Duffy, who flees from the woman with whom he had been cultivating an intimate relationship at the instant when her touch prepared for a consummation of intimacy; like Gabriel, in "The Dead," whose desire for Gretta subsides when he is alone with her, the urge for self-defeat brings the protagonist in "Araby" to a final repudiation of what he had seemed to want.

CHAPTER II

The Broken Harmonium:
Paralysis as Celibacy

IN "Eveline," "Clay," and "A Painful Case," Joyce describes a disintegration of the personality like that D. H. Lawrence discusses in *Psychoanalysis and the Unconscious*:

> A soul cannot come into its own through that love alone which is unison. If it stresses the one mode, the sympathetic mode, beyond a certain point, it breaks its own integrity, and corruption sets in in the living organism. On both planes of love, upper and lower, the two modes must act complementary to one another, the sympathetic and the separatist. It is the absolute failure to see this that has torn the modern world into two halves, the one half warring for the voluntary, objective, separatist control, the other for the pure sympathetic. The individual psyche divided against itself divides the world against itself, and an unthinkable progress of calamity ensues unless there be a reconciliation.[1]

The protagonists in *Dubliners* dwell in either of the halves of Lawrence's divided world, but in each story a tension derives from their attraction to the other half. However, they are incapable of the personal integrity Lawrence sees as a normative condition of human life, the polarity within the individual balancing the "sympathetic" and the "separatist." In "Eveline," "Clay," and "A Painful Case," as usual, Joyce portrays characters alike in having chosen

[1] D. H. Lawrence, *Psychoanalysis and the Unconscious* (New York, 1962), pp. 40–41.

celibacy as a state of life, differing according to their preference for one of the halves of the split world Lawrence discerns. Eveline draws back from Frank because (on the most superficial level) her soul stresses the "sympathetic mode," determined by her memory of a dead mother. In "Clay" Maria is also doomed to celibacy because of a buried identification with a long ago figure. Mr. Duffy, in "A Painful Case," frantically preserves his celibate life because he has given himself over to the other half of Lawrence's dichotomy. He fights "for the voluntary, objective, separatist control," and he wars against "the sympathetic mode" into which his soul would be drawn. On the face of it he is a "gnomon" because he cannot get the two together.

Of all the stories "Eveline" is the most precise characterization of spiritual paralysis. After her mother's death, Eveline, brutally and unjustly treated by her dissolute father, plans escape from Dublin to Buenos Aires with a young sailor, but, for reasons not immediately apparent, she cannot bring herself to board the ship which will take them to a new life. It is in Eveline's inability to escape from her unhappy environment that paralysis is found. This inability stems from a reluctance to embark on an adventure which, at the same time, she pretends to desire. The conflict in the story between her wish to escape an unbearable environment and her attachment to that environment is resolved by the paralysis which stems from neurotic involvement with the past. The story is one of the most painful in *Dubliners*, for it depicts both her desire for liberation and her inability to choose it effectively.

As with the boy in "The Sisters," Eveline is literally enchanted, which accounts for the hypnotic behavior she cannot escape. Though inclined towards freedom, she must finally acquiesce in a slavish sympathy with her dead mother: "As she mused the pitiful vision of her mother's life laid its spell on the very quick of her being" (p. 40). And, although terrified by the vision of her mother's final insanity, she does not avoid a mysterious commitment to the same fate, for at the story's end, "passive, like a helpless animal," she turns her face against Frank, who would save her, and "her eyes gave him no sign of love or farewell or recognition" (p. 41). She reverts to the depressive masochism which is a more descriptive word than "paralysis" for the condition of the Dubliner. The true object of Eveline's quest is a vengeful self-annihilation.

The story is told as though from her point of view but not, as in the first three stories, in the first person. Her identity had been so thoroughly subsumed that she could think of herself only as an object which, in context, indeed she is, being borne off like one of the "brown baggages" carried by the soldiers on the quay (p. 40). Furthermore, though she appears singlemindedly given to rudimentary perceptions, the account of her predicament results as much from a hypnotic lack of identity as from mental incapacity. Her mind works like that of the old pervert in "An Encounter" who gave "the impression that he was repeating something which he had learned by heart or that, magnetized by some words of his own speech, his mind was slowly circling round and round in the same orbit." This quality of hypnotic interior monologue is conveyed in her tortuous approach to the choice presented her: "She had consented to go away, to leave her home. Was that wise? She tried to weigh each side of the question. In her home anyway she had shelter and food; she had those whom she had known all her life about her. Of course she had to work hard both in the house and at business. What would they say of her in the Stores when they found out that she had run away with a fellow? Say she was a fool, perhaps; and her place would be filled up by advertisement" (p. 37). Eveline's self-perception rests almost totally on what she imagines others think of her or would think of her, illustrating one very disturbing effect of *Dubliners*. Joyce has depicted shells of personality who exert little or no force of being on themselves or on those around them except in a negative way. Eveline is the most extreme example.

It is enlightening here to contrast this story with Lawrence's "The Fox," which has similar circumstances, with a different outcome.[2] In that story, Henry Grenfel, a soldier on leave, visits a farm inhabited by two lesbians, Ellen March and Jill Banford with Jill in the dominant role. The soldier falls in love with Ellen and, in order to break up the lesbian relationship he murders Jill Banford by what appears to be an accident. He leaves the farm with Ellen, a Midland equivalent to Eveline. Though, despite her liberation Ellen remains unhappy as the story ends, there is promise for her eventual regeneration. In Lawrence's story the "savior" figure is at least physically efficacious, as is the case among that long list of male "savior" figures throughout Lawrence. But in "Eveline," as with practically all of Joyce's "Christ" figures, Frank proves finally ineffective. Although Eveline thinks that "Frank would save her. He would give her life," he is powerless in the end. She does not heed his call to her to follow him beyond the "barrier." He does not save her anymore than Joyce could save his fellow Dubliners in his role as aesthetic priest, for although he called to his compatriots from "beyond the barrier," their faces were set against him. Described as sitting by the window recalling her past and imagining her future, Eveline may even manufacture the end of her story: she may never actually even show up for her rendezvous with Frank, but may be putting an imaginative end to it in her chair which goes nowhere, a fitting symbol for the static fantasies of Dublin.[3]

"Eveline" is a remarkably subtle and concise characterization of the way paralysis works. Joyce demonstrates this through an early form of interior monologue. The key to the first three stories was in the identification of the protagonists with adult figures who had "laid a spell on the quick of [their] beings." Even in "Araby," in which this element is least obvious, the boy identified with the priest who had died in the house at the end of the street. As in "The Sisters," and "An Encounter," it is a surrogate identification. But in

---

[2] D. H. Lawrence, *Four Short Novels* (New York, 1965).

[3] For the suggestion that Eveline imagines the end of this story, I am indebted to one of my graduate students, Miss Shelley Sorani.

"Eveline" the original parental incorporation is clear, for Eveline exists chiefly in relation with her parents, unable to attach herself even through surrogate identification with Frank, despite her "confused" delight at being called his "poppens." For this reason she lacks the capacity for enlightenment which marks the more sophisticated protagonists in the first three stories, where the use of first person narration suggests an awareness not found in Eveline, who thinks of herself not as "I" but as "she." At the end of the story, she surrenders (actually or imaginatively) to a state of animal-like paralysis distinct from the more conscious, and therefore more human awareness of the earlier protagonists.

Despite a slavish identification with her parents, for a while Eveline thinks of herself as at least possibly separate from them. She considers severing herself from her early environment, in which role she thinks of her father as a sadistic tyrant: "she sometimes felt herself in danger of her father's violence" (p. 38). Her father would destroy her, but Frank, his opposite, would give her life, and therefore she imagines that if she were his wife, "people would treat her with respect" (p. 37). But the reflections on her savior disperse as she thinks again of her father. However, now the edges of his tyranny blunt as he merges in her imagination with the dead mother: "Another day, when their mother was alive, they had all gone for a picnic to the Hill of Howth. She remembered her father putting on her mother's bonnet to make the children laugh" (p. 39). The image of her father wearing the mother's bonnet disposes Eveline for a final stage of recollection in which gradually and subtly Joyce conveys the power exercised over her by her dead mother, which insinuates itself into her consciousness on the sound of a street organ: "She knew the air. Strange that it should come that very night to remind her of the promise to her mother, her promise to keep the home together as long as she could. . . . As she mused the pitiful vision of her mother's life laid a spell on the very quick of her being—that life of commonplace sacrifices ending in final craziness. She trembled as she heard again her mother's voice saying constantly with foolish insistence: "Derevaun Seraun! Derevaun Seraun!" (p. 40).

According to W. Y. Tindall, Patrick Henchy of the National Library in Dublin has conjectured that this phrase is corrupt Gaelic for "the end of pleasure is pain."[4] The late Professor Roland Smith of the University of Illinois concluded that it is possibly a corruption of the Gaelic, *"Deireadh Amrain Siabran,–ain,"* which means "the end of song is raving madness." A lesser possibility was that of the corrupted Gaelic, *"Deireadh Fuinn S. mearaide,"* which could mean either that "the end of a song," or "the end of inordinate desire" is "the first cloud of insanity." These meanings, particularly "the end of song is raving madness" would all be appropriate to the story. This last expression would clearly tie in with Eveline's having been taken by Frank to see *The Bohemian Girl,* and with his having sung to her about "the lass that loves a sailor" (p. 39). Professor Smith pointed out to me the recurrence in Gaelic of pessimistic proverbs, such as: "Sorrow is laughter's daughter"; "Today we sing, tomorrow we weep"; "His evening song and morning song are not both alike." Any of these expressions would constitute an appropriate epigraph on *Dubliners.*

Balfe's sentimental opera, *The Bohemian Girl,* serves as an appropriate form for Eveline's unsophisticated fantasies about life away from Dublin's secure if pedestrian pieties. She would have imagined herself into the gaudy plight of Arline, daughter to a Count, kidnapped as an infant by Devilshoof, chief of a gypsy tribe, and raised as a gypsy. Twelve years later, her father visits the gypsy tribe, recognizes her, reestablishes her in his court—gives her to the faithful Thaddeus, a Polish exile who loves her. They achieve a comic liaison despite the attempted vengeance of the evil gypsy queen. Surely Eveline's vision of bohemian life has the character of a comic opera, where villains and heroes are clearly defined and where the end of song is not raving madness but another song: a lover's harmony:

[4] W. Y. Tindall, *A Reader's Guide to James Joyce* (New York, 1959), p. 22.

> Ne'er should the soul over sorrows grieve,
> With which the bosom hath ceased to heave;
> Ne'er should we think of the tempest past,
> If we reach the haven at last.[5]

But, the actualities of Dublin have provided Eveline with a much more complicated vision of good and evil. Her father may be a Devilshoof; but he is also an affectionate comic-opera Count. She may be a bohemian girl, but she is also a gypsy queen, devoted to an ineffectual revenge.

Like the earlier stories, "Eveline" contains a thinly veiled sexuality, with the suggestion of incestuous perversity and sexual sado-masochism. So close is the relationship between sex and pain that both concepts are suggested in several places through the same imagery; the father's "blackthorn stick" is both an instrument of threatened punishment and a symbol of incestuous desire: "he had begun to threaten her and say what he would do to her only for her dead mother's sake" (p. 38). Though we learn that her father had not actually chastised her, he had "gone for" her brothers when they were growing up, and the first mention of the father in the story occurs on the opening page when Eveline recalls that "Her father used often to hunt them in out of the field with his black-thorn stick" (p. 36). Eveline's struggle to preserve herself against him expresses itself in the defense of her virginity: on market day she holds "her black leather purse tightly in her hand" (p. 38). Here is an implicit autoeroticism that is both a defense against her father and a surrogate for the sexual relation with him she unconsciously desires.

Eveline's attitude towards the erotic is determined not only by the living threat of her father, but by identification with her dead mother, for she is ever conscious of the effects on her mother of a brutal marriage. "She would not be treated as her mother had been" (p. 37), for that treatment resulted in her mother's illness, "final

[5] *The Bohemian Girl*, music by M. W. Balfe, libretto by A. Bunn (New York, 185[?]), p. 32.

craziness," and death, and this end came as a result of a "life of commonplace *sacrifices*" (p. 40). The mother was a victim, sacrificed to her husband, which resulted in her derangement (like that of the priest in "The Sisters," and of the pervert in "An Encounter"). Because of this identification, compounded with a repressed desire for her father, Eveline is incapable of a sexual relationship with Frank, an inability symbolically expressed in the last lines of the story:

> A bell clanged upon her heart. She felt him seize her hand:
> —Come!
> All the seas of the world tumbled about her heart. He was drawing her into them: he would drown her. She gripped with both hands at the iron railing.
> —Come!
> No! No! No! It was impossible. Her hands clutched the iron in frenzy. Amid the seas she sent a cry of anguish!
> —Eveline! Evvy!
> He rushed beyond the barrier and called to her to follow. He was shouted at to go on but he still called to her. She set her white face to him, passive, like a helpless animal. Her eyes gave him no sign of love or farewell or recognition. (p. 41)

Eveline's inability to enter the ship with Frank implies her repression of sexual feeling: the vision of her inability to give herself to Frank prevents her from entering the ship. The feeling that she would be "drowned" (as her mother had been) by a relationship with a man who, although unlike her father, is identified with him in some way, causes her to fear death, annihilation in "all the seas of the world."

And yet the decision to remain at home leads also to annihilation and death. She has misplaced the object of her fear, withdrawing from Frank as though he would destroy her, and choosing instead destruction at the hands of her tyrannical father. Her rejection of Frank would seem to be a sadomasochistic pose by which she can rationalize the satisfaction of a repressed desire to be seduced and destroyed by her father.

The religious theme of "Eveline," no less than the erotic, resembles that in "The Sisters" in which an underlying irony is the failure of Christ in His mission of redemption. "Eveline" suggests that the promises of Christ, which according to Catholic tradition were made to Margaret Mary Alacoque, have not been fulfilled. This idea appears by association of the colored print of the promises with the "broken harmonium" near which it is placed, and by the promises themselves, for their content contrasts sharply with Eveline's situation.[6]

Marvin Magalaner poses a question about the appearance of St. Margaret Mary Alacoque in "Eveline," asking whether "Joyce intended any identification of the saint with Eveline."[7] Margaret Mary (1647–1690), a religious of the Visitation Order in France, was a celibate who at one time briefly returned to "the world" (to

---

[6] The promises of the Sacred Heart are as follows: "(1) I will give them [i.e. the faithful who display in their homes a representation of the Sacred Heart and who receive the Eucharist on first Fridays of each month] all the graces necessary in their state of life. (2) I will establish peace in their homes. (3) I will comfort them in all their afflictions. (4) I will be their secure refuge during life, and above all in death. (5) I will bestow abundant blessings on all their undertakings. (6) Sinners shall find in My Heart the source and the infinite ocean of mercy. (7) Tepid souls shall become fervent. (8) Fervent souls shall quickly mount to high perfection. (9) I will bless every place in which an image of My Heart shall be exposed and honored. (10) I will give to priests the gift of touching the most hardened hearts. (11) Those who shall promote this devotion shall have their names written in My Heart never to be effaced. (12) I promise thee in the excessive mercy of My Heart that My all powerful love will grant to all those who communicate on the First Friday in nine consecutive months the grace of final perseverence; they shall not die in my disgrace nor without receiving their Sacraments. My Divine Heart shall be their safe refuge in this last moment."

Certain stories in *Dubliners* seem ironical commentaries on individual promises: especially noteworthy is the relationship between the following stories and corresponding promises, indicated by number after the title: "Grace": 1, 6, 7, 10; "Eveline" :2, 3, 4, 5, 9; "Counterparts": 1, 2, 5; "The Sisters": 4, 6, 7, 10.

[7] Marvin Magalaner, *Time of Apprenticeship: The Fiction of Young James Joyce* (New York, 1959), pp. 152–153.

be returned to her convent by the vision of a reproachful and suffering Christ), just as Eveline had contemplated escape from her celibacy in Dublin. Furthermore, Margaret Mary at another time in her life became paralyzed as the result of self-imposed penances, a condition of which she was miraculously cured.[8] Eveline is spiritually and physically paralyzed at the end of the story. And Eveline, like Margaret Mary, has her "savior," for she thinks of Frank in just those terms. "He would save her" (p. 40). Just as Margaret Mary was cured of her paralysis, Eveline could be cured of hers if she could submit to the "salvation" of love, a submission against which she inhibits herself. Eveline ends up ultimately without love. Her celibacy was fruitless, her final lot, living death.

Even supposing that Joyce intended such an association, the story is even more complex; the analogy divides to include an opposite meaning. As Margaret Mary returned to her celibate life at the vision of a sorrowful Christ, Eveline returns to her celibacy in response to the vision of her sorrowful, "sacrificed" mother. She turns away from Frank who "would save her" from her mother's fate, to the image of her mother who would save her from entering the "black mass" of the ship and life with Frank. Her mother saves her from a life of erotic sacrifice with Frank for a life of "commonplace" sacrifice. Her mother saves Eveline from what she can only envision as death for a fate which, under the aspect of dutiful "life" is really death. Eveline finally rejects freedom under the aspect of bondage and turns back to bondage under the aspect of freedom.

The story apparently presents Eveline as a masochist who has rejected her own chances for life. But, when we give a thought to Frank it is clear that Eveline behaves sadistically to him. Left to go to Buenos Aires alone, he is punished instead of her father, the real culprit. Her behavior can only be adequately described as sado-masochistic. She gets revenge on Frank by identifying with his discomfiture as she also identifies with her mother's victimization,

[8] *Catholic Encyclopedia*, vol. 9 (New York, 1907–1912), p. 653.

both in her imagination and in the life circumstances she finally chooses. Typically, most of these complicated maneuvers can be accomplished in her imagination: she hardly needs to leave her chair. Therefore, even her refusal to enter the ship with Frank she may only imagine as she sits by her window, the odor of dusty cretonne an appropriate cancellation of the "good airs" of South America which Frank would have her breathe. In *Dubliners,* no one ever behaves with simple masochism: always there is a sadist component which usually holds the upper hand. For example, with adolescent delight, the boy in "The Sisters," had participated in the final corruption of the old priest; also, he subtly torments the old aunts by refusing their meager offerings of biscuit and wine. The narrator of "Araby" will return empty-handed from the bazaar, contrary to his chivalric promise of a ritual gift. No one ever behaves with simple masochism because there is no such phenomenon.

One can think of Maria in "Clay" as a grown-up Eveline in Joyce's scripture, just as the Virgin Mary is regarded traditionally as a "new Eve." Maria is a projection of what becomes of the lower-class Dublin woman frustrated in love by her own inhibitions, and that of course describes her precursor, Eveline. Employed in the kitchen of a laundry, Maria takes the hallowe'en holiday with her brother and his family, and, as part of a game, blindfolded, she chooses a dish of clay jokingly substituted by her brother's children: afterwards she sings a song by Balfe, omitting the second verse. In "Clay," one encounters a quest so deeply repressed that it is only implied through symbolic details. At first, Maria seems not to be looking for anything so much as she is attempting to preserve her status quo; she gives an impression of smug complacency: "she looked with quaint affection at the dimunitive body which she had so often adorned. In spite of its years she found it a nice tidy little body" (p. 101). Joyce hints that for all of her complacent "peace-making," Maria is a dual personality: a typical Joycean woman—a madonna, and a witch.[9] Consequently Maria both in name and function appears as a "veritable peace-maker," a Blessed Virgin figure. But, as Magalaner has observed, she looks like a witch, and the story takes place on the night when witches are free.[10] She is neither a pre-Raphaelite innocent, nor a Romantic *femme fatale*, but a grotesque parody of ethereal exoticism, devoid even of the physical attractiveness of many of Joyce's other women: not a Circe but a hag with a celestial aura. Therefore her integrity is not integrity and the wholeness of her virginity, only apparent. By her own standards she brims with unvirginal desires. Both her superficially virginal integrity and underlying opposition to virginity are seen in the tea rings which "seemed uncut; but if you went closer you would see that they had been cut into long thick even slices" (p. 99). Though the ring symbolizes wholeness, here the rings are actually cut and ready to distribute.[11]

The barmbrack is a symbolic extension of Maria—in distributing the barmbrack she gives herself away (or leaves herself behind, as with the plumcake on the tram), although on the surface she looks whole, just as the tea rings "seemed uncut." Underlying her smugness is a queasy ferment of repression. She would both remain in

[9] The concept of Maria as a witch is also developed by Richard Carpenter and Daniel Leary, "The Witch Maria," *James Joyce Review* 3, nos. 1 and 2 (February, 1959): 3–7. Magalaner's insight, on which this article was based, was, in turn, suggested to him by Leonard Albert, who proposed the idea in "James Joyce and the New Psychology," Ph.D. dissertation (New York, 1957), p. 215.

[10] Maria may also be a "Punch" figure, in appearance anyway, as F. X. Mathews argues. "Punchestime: A New Look at 'Clay,'" *James Joyce Quarterly* 4, no. 2 (Winter, 1967); 102–106. He does not really get around the problem that Punch is masculine.

[11] For Brewster Ghiselin, the barmbrack, cut and ready for distribution, is "an intimation of the [sacramental] host, divided before the ritual and mechanically apportioned." "The Unity of Joyce's *Dubliners*," *Accent* 16 (1956): 203. This insight fits in with the concept of a Maria who, as a "heavenly being," participates in "celestial mysteries." The comparison of the ring of barmbrack to the Eucharist also parallels Maria's being one and divided, with and without integrity. The Eucharist remains sacramentally one however much the host is divided.

possession of herself and give herself away, so that although "she thought how much better it was to be independent and to have your own money in your pocket" (p. 102), shortly afterwards she recalls "how confused the gentleman with the greyish moustache had made her" (p. 103). Joyce had used "confused" in "An Encounter" to suggest the boy's notion about green-eyed sailors, with the erotic connotation to which I referred earlier. In "Eveline," the young girl "always felt pleasantly confused" when Frank sang to her. Little Chandler, in "A Little Cloud," blushes constantly and looks "confusedly" after Ignatius Gallaher's erotic suggestiveness (p. 79). The recurring use of the word in reference to hinted sexuality points to Maria's "confusion" as the irruption into consciousness of her repression, and the function of this repressed desire. It threatens to disturb the carefully structured pattern of Maria's conscious, and false, behavior. Therefore the man on the tram had made her "confused." In reply to Stanislaus's question about the "Dublin by Lamplight Laundry" where Maria works, Joyce explained: "The phrase . . . means that Dublin by Lamplight is a wicked place full of wicked and lost women whom a kindly committee gathers together for the good work of washing my dirty shirts. I like the phrase because 'it is a gentle way of putting it.' "[12] Maria works in a home for reformed Magdalens, which is not to suggest that Joyce is implying she is a reformed prostitute. In "Clay" we are only told that her brothers got her a "position" at the laundry because their home had broken up (p. 100). But we are also told that she "liked it" there; the Protestant supervisors are "very nice people," the surroundings are pleasant. Perhaps also she finds the other women are her sisters under the skin. Though unconscious, her behavior on the tram might correspond to the more obvious enticements of a Dublin whore.

The schizophrenic parts of Maria's character emerge more clearly when examined separately and they require explanation in terms of the theme of "Clay," and in relation to the other stories, especial-

[12] Joyce to Stanislaus Joyce, 13 November 1906, *Letters*, vol. 2, p. 192.

ly "Eveline." Maria is a parody of the Virgin Mary. Her role as a "peace-maker," as Magalaner notes, suggests that "Joyce intended to build a rough analogy between the laundry worker Maria and the Virgin Mary."[13] "Maria" is, of course, the Church's title for Mary in Latin. Also, she is a virgin with children, as Magalaner observes, for she had nursed her brothers Alphy and Joe.[14] Furthermore, "Joe used often to say:—Mama is mamma, but Maria is my proper mother" (p. 100). In "Clay" also appears the purse symbol which had appeared in "Eveline" in a similar context. "She took out her purse with the silver clasps and read again the words *A Present from Belfast*. She was very fond of that purse because Joe had brought it to her five years before when he and Alphy had gone to Belfast on a Whit-Monday trip" (p. 100). As in "Eveline" the purse implies virginity, but, because Maria's virginity has a "sacred" quality, the purse is closed by "silver clasps," and it was brought to her after a "Whit-Monday trip" which suggests the Holy Spirit by whom Mary conceived without losing virginal integrity.

However, despite the comparison with Mary, Maria's witchlike quality is indicated not only by her freedom on Hallowe'en but by her physical appearance: "Maria was a very, very small person indeed but she had a very long nose and a very long chin" (p. 99).

Perceiving "Clay" as a continuation of the story of Eveline helps clarify the holy virgin–haglike witch combination of Maria's character, and points to the thematic unity in *Dubliners*. Eveline's tendency toward sexual self-expression has been converted into the neurotic cunning of Maria who still desires what Eveline once appeared to want. But these desires she has repressed under a cover of "demure nods and hems" (p. 103). They show in acts such as leaving the plumcake on a tram next to a talkative gentleman. She really leaves herself with him, but because her desire to do so is repressed

[13] Marvin Magalaner, "The Other Side of James Joyce," *Arizona Quarterly* 9 (Spring, 1953): 8.
[14] *Ibid.*

she forgets her "slip" until later, when she attributes it to having
been "confused," a frequent euphemism for "sexually aroused" in
Dubliners.

That Maria is a grown-up Eveline is further suggested by Joyce's
intention to treat of his subject matter in the categories of youth,
adolescence, maturity, and public life: of these Joyce himself placed
"Eveline" in the category of adolescence, "Clay" in that of maturity.[15] Though "mature," Maria had failed to choose life.[16] She had
long-ago repressed her real desires as an evil, rather than an unre-
pressed, sacrifice of the good implicit in sincere virginity; repression has left her smug but unsatisfied.

In "Clay" the song that Maria sings refers to the past in much
the same way as the darkened hall in "Araby." Both the song and
the hall are symbols which occur at the end of the story. Both signify
attempts to reach the past, and in both there is the element of blotting out the past, for the boy arrives finally at a darkened hall, and
Maria omits a painfully significant verse from Balfe's song. The
darkness of the hall is a shadow from the past blotting out what the
boy pretends to seek. A similar shadow falls on the memory of
Maria, causing her unconsciously deliberate slip. Both sought in
the past what could not be, and both are in some way aware of the
illusion. The significant difference is in the degree to which they
are conscious of the illusion, for the boy experiences self-derision
at the vanity of his attempt, but Maria appears consciously unaware
of her error. Consequently, while the boy in "Araby" achieves a
degree of awareness, Maria does not—the reader alone realizes the

[15] Richard Ellmann, *James Joyce* (New York, 1959), p. 216. Corroboration
of this comes from Leonard Albert who thinks that " 'Eveline' " may have
been a preliminary study for the more ambitious story of the virginal laundress
Maria." Albert, "James Joyce and the New Psychology," pp. 236–237.

[16] The theme of "death in life" in "Clay" is pointed out by Richard B.
Hudson in "Joyce's 'Clay,' " *The Explicator* 6 (March, 1948): Item 30. Hudson
is also aware of "her subconscious longing for marriage and children," as indicated for example by "her confusion as a result of the old man's error on the
tram."

extent of her self-deception. She deceives herself by altering the past in her imagination, an act expertly represented by the song she sings, which significantly recounts a dream:

> I dreamt that I dwelt in marble halls
> With vassals and serfs at my side,
> And of all who assembled within those walls
> That I was the hope and the pride.
>
> I had riches too great to count; could boast
> Of a high ancestral name,
> But I also dreamt, which pleased me most
> That you loved me still the same. (p. 106)

As in "Eveline," Joyce uses Balfe's *Bohemian Girl* to define the paralytic frustration of his character. In the opera, Arline, still a gypsy girl, sings the song to Thaddeus, who, unknown to her, had saved her life when she was a child threatened by a wounded stag at her father's chateau. Her dream was of course a true image of her childhood, and she is restored to her rightful dignity by the end of the opera. The verse Maria omits from her rendition of the song, refers in the opera to the undying affection held for Arline by Thaddeus, which culminates in their coming together in the last scene:

> I dream'd that suitors besought my hand,
> That knights upon bended knee,
> And with vows no maiden heart could withstand
> That they pledged their faith to me.
> And I dream'd that one of this noble host
> Came forth my hand to claim;
> Yet I also dream'd, which charmed me most,
> That you loved me still the same.[17]

Arline's dream obviously opposes the reality of Maria's life. If she is a grown-up Eveline, the omitted last verse would refer to her

---

[17] "The Gipsy Girl's Dream," *The Bohemian Girl*, p. 15.

earlier rejection of a suitor who had made vows which her heart had been able to withstand: for Maria a memory fraught with pain and, perhaps, in view of her superficial smugness, an element of spinsterish relief. She still has, after all, her nice, tidy little body intact, even if her wishes are not quite so tidy.[18] And yet, like the typical Dubliner (as in "Ivy Day in the Committee Room," "The Dead," etc.), Maria romanticizes the past, a fiction summed up by Maria's brother Joe when he says after her song, "there was no time like the long ago" (p. 106). No such thing ever existed as the "long ago" of the Dubliner's imagination. Consequently Joe's tears for a fictional past blind him from "finding" anything in the present: "his eyes filled up so much with tears that he could not find what he was looking for and in the end he had to ask his wife to tell him where the corkscrew was" (p. 106).

"Clay" captures a frequent pose of the Dubliner: the intolerable present results from an intolerable past. But instead of trying to change his present state, the Dubliner tries to convince himself that the past was not only tolerable but so glorious that the present will never measure up to it. He alters the past because he cannot bring himself to believe that he rejected life; to believe this would be not to exist.

In "Clay," Joe and Maria are blind about themselves. Mr. Duffy, in "A Painful Case," experiences somewhat more self-enlightenment. The admitted model for Mr. Duffy, Stanislaus Joyce

[18] Richard Hudson regards the omission as Maria's conscious or unconscious rejection of "such a direct statement of her own situation." Hudson, "Joyce's 'Clay,'" Item 30. Marvin Magalaner sees her error as the result of an emotional block which prevents her from voicing remarks "at variance with the reality of her dull life" (p. 13). Wm. T. Noon, S.J. seems to be aware only of the conscious side of Maria; consequently he says that Joyce is portraying Maria as "a modern work-a-day saint," and therefore her error is the result of her saintlike wisdom: "It would not be wise to expose herself to ridicule by singing the second verse." "Joyce's 'Clay': An Interpretation," *College English* 17 (November, 1955): 93–95. My analysis is obviously not in accord with Father Noon's opinion: sanctity is irreconcilable with the kind of self-deception operating in Maria. I cannot imagine Joyce seriously presenting in Maria a portrait of sanctity.

indicated clearly the relationship between this story and "Clay" when he wrote in *My Brother's Keeper* that "Mr. Duffy is the type of the male celibate, as Maria in 'Clay' is of the female celibate."[19] As there is evidence that "Clay" is a projection of what a person like Eveline was to become, so "A Painful Case" was intended by Joyce to be, in the words of Stanislaus, "a portrait of what my brother imagined I should become in middle age."[20] Joyce displays a practice frequent in *Dubliners*, the projecting on a fictional screen of the fortunes of both real and fictional persons, according to certain potentialities he saw in them. As the boy in "An Encounter" idly chewed "one of those green stems on which girls tell fortunes," he first saw the old pervert who gradually turned into a vision of what the boy was to become. Nothing could be more indicative of Joyce's concept of himself as standing apart from his creation like God, for whom past, present, and future are one, although they are distinct in creation itself. The past, present, and future are distinct in *Dubliners*, although united in the instant of artistic gestation. By the writing of *Finnegans Wake*, these temporal distinctions have been obliterated: all past time is the present—Finn Macool is Finnegan, everybody comes with H. C. Earwicker, and they all come at the same time. *Dubliners* is as much a potential *Finnegans Wake* as it is on the verge of becoming *Ulysses*.[21]

Therefore, it is not surprising to discover that in "A Painful Case," as in other stories, the past operates in the present. Because of attitudes and emotions earlier repressed Duffy is bound to act as he does though he seems unaware of the springs of his behavior. This pattern can be demonstrated in the story from a careful examination of Joyce's portrayal of Duffy's actions in the present.

[19] Stanislaus Joyce, *My Brother's Keeper* (New York, 1958), p. 159.

[20] *Ibid.*, p. 160. However, Marvin Magalaner feels that much more of James than of Stanislaus is to be found in Mr. Duffy. Magalaner, *Time of Apprenticeship*, p. 88.

[21] Richard Levin and Charles Shattuck conclude that "many of the characters, devices, themes, actions [of *Dubliners*] are anticipations of similar things in Joyce's *Ulysses* and are to be studied in a genetic relationship." "First Flight to Ithaca," *Accent* 4 (Winter, 1944): 75–99.

In "A Painful Case" Joyce constructs ironic tragedy from the raw material of melodrama. A bachelor who has successfully isolated himself from other people, Mr. Duffy meets at a concert a married woman, neglected by her husband. They develop a relationship Duffy wishes to think strictly spiritual until, one evening, Mrs. Sinico touches his hand, an intimacy from which Duffy vehemently recoils. He breaks off with her, only to discover several years later that she had turned to drink and had thrown herself in front of a train. Stunned, Duffy gradually realizes his responsibility for her degradation and death, but the story ends with a return to his previous sense of thorough isolation. Stanislaus Joyce himself thought the story "too big for the form you use."[22] He was then reading *Anna Karenina*,[23] which treats at length a similar theme—the suicide of an adulterous woman rejected by her lover. But the obtuseness of Joyce's brother shows through here: apparently he did not perceive that in comparison with Tolstoy, who elevated low mimetic fiction to high tragedy, his brother was treating low mimetic themes in an ironic fashion. Tragedy in a Tolstoyan sense was simply not possible in Joyce's Dublin. Of his appreciation of Tolstoy, James Joyce wrote in detail to his brother.[24] But he did not follow his practice completely because Tolstoyan Russia was not Joycean Ireland. "A Painful Case" is the story of an inability to sustain a masculine passion. *Anna Karenina* recounts the long drawn out evocation, satisfaction, and final tedium of a passion. The long novel was a form appropriate to the depiction of an intense passion, with its growth, climax, and eventual quiescence. The short story form appears especially appropriate for Joyce's meticulous depiction of Dublin's incapacity for spiritual action. Joyce

[22] Stanislaus Joyce to Joyce, 10 October 1905, *Letters*, vol. 2, p. 115.

[23] "I am reading 'Anna Karenina' at present. You say Tolstoy is never dull, never tired. He makes other people dull and tired, and that's a damn sight worse." *Ibid.*, p. 119.

[24] "As for Tolstoy, I disagree with you altogether. Tolstoy is a magnificent writer. He is never dull, never stupid, never tired, never pedantic, never theatrical! He is head and shoulders over the others." Joyce to Stanislaus Joyce, 18 September 1905, *Letters*, vol. 2, p. 106.

has been compared less often with Tolstoy than with Chekov, who depicts in a later Russian society paralytic elements similar to those of Joyce's Dublin. An odor of the decay of moral faculties hangs about Chekov's Russian provincial towns and estates as about Joyce's Dublin, redolent, said Joyce, with the odor of offal and ashpits. Of course, Chekov was a master of the short story form in which since there was seldom extensive "action," either physical or moral, there was seldom a need to treat anything at length. His plays are of a more conventional length, but their themes are similar to those in Joyce stories. Uncle Vanya, who returns at last to his dreary celibacy and tedious ledger-keeping, after an abortive fling at the grand passion, resembles James Duffy. His sister, who joins him in his passive acquiescence, recalls Joyce's Eveline. The chief difference in tone is that Chekov preserves for his characters a melancholy compassion, tempered by a gentle humor; Joyce is short on compassion, long on wit, his perceptions harsher and funnier, but also gloomier.

Duffy's inevitable return to habitual loneliness imbues the story with the same circular quality suggested by the behavior of Patrick Morkan's horse in "The Dead," and looks forward to the cyclical character of *Finnegans Wake* which moves toward its end with Anna Livia's sigh that she is "loonely in . . . loneness," and of which the last sentence continues on the first page, with its bawdy reference to Tristan's "penisolate" war. Mr. Duffy's habits have not really changed at the end of the story, except perhaps to be more deeply ingrained. He was paralyzed at the beginning, and at the end, only more so. When, like Morkan's horse, he had emerged briefly from his daily round of compulsive circularity, the first reminder from the past ("King Billy's statue" in "The Dead") prompted a return to the cycle of old habits. Mr. Duffy retains only a fruitless insight into what life could have been. The nature of these habits, how they operate in the present, and something of their cause can be deduced from a consideration of certain details from "A Painful Case."

As with Maria in "Clay," there is not apparently the element of conscious "quest" about this story. Until his meeting with Mrs. Sinico, Mr. Duffy seems neither to be looking for anything nor attempting or even desiring escape from his present circumstances, although they are in themselves ordered to his escape from society. Like Maria in "Clay," he has achieved a *status quo*, which it is his major effort to preserve. He has lived eremitically in Chapelizod, because "he wished to live as far as possible from the city" (p. 107), and he ate where he "felt himself safe from the society of Dublin's gilded youth" (p. 109). His orderly and austerely furnished room reflects monkish habits, an abhorrence of "anything which betokened physical or mental disorder" (p. 108). The arrangement of his library suggests the nature of his devotion to culture: "a complete Wordsworth stood at one end of the lowest shelf and a copy of the *Maynooth Catechism* . . . stood at one end of the top shelf" (pp. 107–108). The arrangement implies the romantically lyrical basis of a character governed by a dogmatic conscience, an incongruity of which he is ironically aware enough to append an advertisement for *Bile Beans* to a notebook of his own epigrams.

Finally, although Mr. Duffy wants to escape from other people, and thus in some way from the reality of life, Joyce emphasizes his honesty. Suburbs other than Chapelizod he dislikes because they are "pretentious" (p. 107). He dined at an eating-house "where there was a certain plain honesty in the bill of fare" (p. 109). This honesty disposes him for the insight he has at the story's end concerning his own plight; but honesty is not enough.

Nothing happens until Mr. Duffy's accidental meeting with Mrs. Sinico at a concert, for up to this point Joyce has given a detailed exposition of Duffy's character. Unlike the earlier stories, the plot of "A Painful Case" develops from an encounter not deliberately sought by the protagonist. He has not, like the boy in "An Encounter" gone forth to experience "wild sensations." And yet, though he has ordered his whole life to self-isolation, Duffy does not at first recoil from Mrs. Sinico, even though it is only after their third encounter by chance that "he found courage to make an appointment" (p. 110). In spite of himself he had been disposed for such a relationship just as his behavior during their affair implies he wished it to end as it did. That he knowingly entered upon such an adventure with a married woman would indicate his foreseeing its limitations.

An analysis of their acquaintance reveals the bizarre quality of his attitude toward her. At first it appears he desired to share with her his intellectual life; but soon he achieves an umbilical dependence on her. "With almost maternal solicitude she urged him to let his nature open to the full; she became his confessor" (p. 110). "Her companionship was like a warm soil about an exotic" (p. 111). Theirs is a relationship without reciprocity. He does not draw her out, inquire into what she thinks. It is on his part a friendship of use. Furthermore, his is a schizoid perception. On the one hand, "this union exalted him, wore away the rough edges of his character, emotionalized his mental life" (p. 111); but as he feels this "affection" he hears his own voice "insisting on the soul's incurable loneliness" (p. 111).

Despite his apparent desire for a purely spiritual relationship, he places himself in circumstances which would lead to a sexual affair. They spend their evenings alone in her cottage, and many times "she allowed the dark to fall upon them, refraining from lighting the lamp" (p. 111). He has done everything to allow a seduction but at the first physical contact (in which she takes the initiative) he abruptly ends their acquaintance. As long as the relationship remains overtly respectable, he can maintain an angelic self-image in what he actually regards as a morally compromising situation; but when this state threatens to become openly immoral, he must stop it. His guilt feelings after Emily's death suggest that he knew what he was doing and didn't know what he was doing. Consequently he experiences contradictory reactions to her death in the alternate evocation of "the two images in which he now conceived her" (p. 116).

Immediately after reading of her death, he is revolted to think

of her having been his "soul's companion" when she has been revealed as vicious, degraded, sullying his angelic spirit. But a little
later he re-experiences her presence imaginatively and this touches
off the other more accurate image. He begins to recall her as a warm
and intelligent woman, the companion of his walks, a person. "Now
that she was gone he understood how lonely her life must have been,
sitting night after night alone in that room" (p. 116). And he thinks,
"Why had he withheld life from her? Why had he sentenced her to
death?" (p. 117). He regards himself as an angel: he even lived "at
a little distance from his body" (p. 108). He lives in *Chapelizod*
in quarters reminiscent of a monk's cell, and reads the account of
her death like a priest reading the Mass (as if he had sacrificed her)
"not aloud, but moving his lips as a priest does when he reads the
prayers *Secreto*" (p. 113). And his first reaction is to affirm the justice of God at her fate.

But this image of himself as a priest, almost a disembodied spirit,
quivers temporarily in a moment of insight when he sees himself
responsible for her death, as an outcast from life's feast, gnawing
"the rectitude of his life" (p. 117). He thinks of her in alternate
images according as he is seeing himself; when he regards himself
as a spirit he condemns her as a fallen woman in relation to him,
and he judges her from his height. But when this self-image is
temporarily disturbed and he sees himself as human, he regards
her also with a mask of human compassion, as someone not to be
judged scornfully. But at last he returns to his previous condition.
"He could not feel her near him in the darkness . . . He felt that he
was alone" (p. 117).

The last two paragraphs of the story reiterate the dualism of his
character. Described at the outset wishing to live as far as possible
from Dublin, he has at the story's end again removed himself from
the city and looks back on it from the crest of Magazine Hill. Having
gained some insight into himself as a result of re-living his acquaintance with Mrs. Sinico in the light of her death, he feels his
isolation acutely: the lights of the city burn "redly and hospitably

in the cold night" (p. 117). He notices furtive lovers nearby in the shadow of the wall of the park and brims with despair. "He felt that he had been outcast from life's feast. One human being had seemed to love him and he had denied her life and happiness: he had sentenced her to ignominy, a death of shame. He knew that the prostrate creatures down by the wall were watching him and wished him gone. No one wanted him; he was outcast from life's feast" (p. 117). One cannot take these sentimental reactions too seriously. A truer note occurs in the next stage of his awareness— a revulsion for the erotic involvement implicit in such communion: the lovers who occasion his despair are engaged in "venal and furtive loves." The goods train "winding . . . like a worm with a fiery head winding through the darkness, obstinately and laboriously" symbolizes his own sexual desire. And this same symbol, the train, dins in his ears a noise repeating "the syllables of her name," with the obvious pun on the repetition of *Sin*-i-co (I co-operated in sin).[25] He feels finally that an invitation to life's feast implies the sinful indulgence with the woman he has killed. This realization returns him to the death-like state of complete repression. "He turned back the way he had come" (p. 117). Duffy turns again into the circle of his previous existence as though his brief contact with life might never have been: "He began to doubt the reality of what memory told him. He halted under a tree and allowed the rhythm to die away. He could not feel her near him in the darkness nor her voice touch his ear. He waited for some minutes listening. He could hear nothing: the night was perfectly silent. He listened again: perfectly silent. He felt that he was alone" (p. 117).

In these last paragraphs are three stages: the first is compounded of insight into his self-imposed isolation with a desire to break out

[25] In the manuscript drafts for this story, Joyce was more explicit: "melody of the engine, 'Emily Sinico, Emily Sinico, Emily Sinico.' " Marvin Magalaner comments that "even the stress marks to indicate the rhythm of the noise of the train are present." Magalaner, *Time of Apprenticeship*, p. 162.

of the circle of his deathlike existence. But in the second stage his feeling that this would necessarily involve illicit indulgence drives him automatically to shut the door against the life which beckons but threatens, and so finally he shuts his ears to reality and returns to his futile circling of the statue of the past.

His rationalization is that since participation in life's feast must be "furtive and venal," because illicit (just as Mrs. Sinico was an illicit object), he must choose what is to him the "purer" part. His final posture is that of an unhappy angel. Yet his selection of an illicit liaison in the first place would indicate that he was defending himself against the involvement with life in a full and satisfying relationship he seems to lament. Perhaps having felt and repressed an earlier rejection, he could by neurotic devices protect himself against the possibility of a later rejection. And so having chosen a forbidden relationship, Duffy later feels outcast because of the hopeless masochism of wanting something which he cannot have. But, like Eveline, he achieves a typical sadistic revenge in the frustration and degradation of another person. Mrs. Sinico's death is Duffy's sadistic pyrrhic victory.

In "A Painful Case" Joyce kept to his intention of creating a conscience for his race and giving the Dubliners a hard look at themselves in the mirror of his art. He must first shatter the false Irish conscience as in Duffy and replace it with one not opposed to life. Consequently, for a while at least, Duffy feels his "moral nature disintegrating," under the influence of more human feelings. That is to say: the sadomasochistic neurosis begins to dissolve. The product of a tyrannical conscience which causes his first reaction to Mrs. Sinico's death to be one of harsh judgment, his "moral nature" opposes life. When his "moral" nature begins to disintegrate for a moment, more gentle and humane feelings briefly emerge, though they are probably no more than a pose. He feels (or pretends) compassion for her and shortly thereafter for himself: he seems moved by an intolerable desire for life and love. Here one discerns a theme reminiscent of Nietzsche, as in *The Genealogy of Morals,* where he assailed the "Christian" antipathy toward life, fostered by the "ascetic priests'" obsession with the "tyranny of such paradoxical and sophistical concepts as *guilt, sin or sinfulness, perdition, damnation.*"[26] The attitude excoriated by Nietzsche parallels that of Duffy's so-called moral nature, resembling that of Nietzsche's "ascetic priests." If Joyce implied that Duffy had been reading Nietzsche since his separation from Mrs. Sinico (and it is after this that the books by Nietzsche are mentioned) perhaps Duffy has been trying to understand this oversevere conscience.[27] Still his first reaction to the news of Mrs. Sinico's death is "Just God," as though his concept of God were simply one of an exacting, punishing God. In order for his feeling for life to emerge, such a God must die.[28]

An underlying theme of "A Painful Case" is the incompatibility of love and justice. If one is "just" he sees with Duffy the pattern of a stern God working out in the lives of those who have transgressed. And if one is himself "just," he can approve, but he cannot also feel compassion or love, for such would be opposed to the conformity with God's designs. Therefore love *must* be illicit, must be opposed to God. And, in the end Duffy cannot assert with Zarathustra that such a fanatic God is dead. In short, he cannot "kill" his own neurosis.[29]

[26] Nietzsche, *The Genealogy of Morals,* trans. Francis Golffing (New York, 1956), p. 265.

[27] In *My Brother's Keeper* Stanislaus says that James added to the story the books by Nietzsche because he was a favorite author of James, not of Stanislaus.

[28] When Nietzsche's Zarathustra goes into the forest he meets a hermit who tells him, "Now I love God: men I do not love. Man is a thing too imperfect for me." But Zarathustra says to himself, "Could it be possible! The old saint in the forest hath not heard of it, that God is dead." *Thus Spoke Zarathustra,* ed. Manuel Komroff (New York, 1936), pp. 2–4. The antithesis is clear: if one pretends to love God he cannot love man because of man's imperfection. If one loves man, he must obliterate God who does not Himself love man but focuses on man only the cold eye of harsh judgment. Love and justice are incompatible.

[29] Marvin Magalaner has contributed a source study of the Nietzschean background of this story. "Joyce, Nietzsche, and Hauptmann in James Joyce's 'A Painful Case," *PMLA* 68 (March, 1953): 95–102.

CHAPTER III

The Gratefully Oppressed: Paralysis as Humiliation

THE SELF-ANNIHILATION of Joyce's Dublin rules the masochistic protagonists in "After the Race," "Two Gallants," "A Little Cloud," and "Counterparts." In the last two stories the protagonists display brief and ineffectual rebelliousness which only serves to ensure Little Chandler and Farrington, like Jimmy Doyle and Lenehan, a more effective paralysis at the end of their adventures than before. Paralyzed in the accomplishments they envy in others, all four achieve an even more depressing awareness of their inferiority. Whether oppressed with eagerness (as in "After the Race" and "Two Gallants"), or resentment (as in "Counterparts" and "A Little Cloud"), the character of oppression invariably grows from a vexation with self, especially by comparison with others, and in each of the stories this oppression takes the form of a vicarious living of alien pursuits. Each is a "gnomon" seeking his missing part through feeling into the experience of others.

"After the Race" openly portrays this degrading parasitism: devoid of self-respect, Jimmy Doyle must feed on that of others. The son of a rich butcher, he accompanies three foreign motorcar enthusiasts as they enter Dublin triumphantly to win an auto race. Later, as a potential investor in their business, he dines with them, accompanies them to the yacht of a rich American where he loses heavily at cards, and at dawn he finds himself stupefied with liquor and with the depression of realizing that he has been used. The

Continentals (particularly the French) win: the Irishman, Jimmy, loses. The story begins with their victory, and ends with his defeat—a paradigm of Ireland's history, cheered by the "gratefully oppressed" Irish.

The first paragraph contrasts the active and passive roles of the Continent and Ireland and foreshadows Jimmy's relationship with his European acquaintances. It reiterates also the relationships between active and passive males, between superiors and inferiors, between victors and the vanquished which occur so often in the other stories: "The cars came scudding in towards Dublin, running evenly like pellets in the groove of the Naas Road. At the crest of of the hill at Inchicore sightseers had gathered in clumps to watch the cars careering homeward and through this channel of poverty and inaction the Continent sped its wealth and industry. Now and again the clumps of people raised the cheer of the gratefully oppressed. Their sympathy, however, was for the blue cars—the cars of their friends, the French" (p. 42). The "wealth and industry" of the Continent appear in the racing car, a symbol of masculinity; Naas Road, a "channel" lined with spectators, represents the "poverty and inaction" of Ireland, and has a symbolic feminine connotation. Irish effeminacy is in awe of masculine prowess, just as further in the story Jimmy's manner expresses "a real respect for foreign accomplishments" (p. 46).

The next paragraph provides a clue for the effeminate passivity of Jimmy, for his sharing the plight of the "gratefully oppressed" Irish: "Séguoin was in good humour because he had unexpectedly received some orders in advance (he was about to start a motor establishment in Paris) and Rivière was in good humour because he was to be appointed manager of the establishment; these two young men (who were cousins) were also in good humor because of the success of the French cars. Villona was in good humor because he had had a very satisfactory luncheon; and besides he was an optimist by nature. The fourth member of the party [Jimmy], however, was too excited to be genuinely happy" (p. 43). Séguoin,

Rivière, and Villona are all in good humour because they have all gotten something they wanted. Despite his sharing in their good fortune, only Jimmy is not "genuinely happy," because he is "too excited." His state approaches the thin line between enjoyment and depression, laughter and tears: by the end of the story this line has been crossed, and he feels glad of the "dark stupor that would cover up his folly" (p. 48). The "excess" of his excitement betrays the pretense of his happiness. He is like the lad in "An Encounter" whose desire for "wild sensations" leads him to the unpleasant vision of himself at his journey's end. Both Dubliners desire the impossible fulfillment of vicarious experience, and consequently they cannot know the feeling of genuine happiness, even as they are apparently in quest of it.

Jimmy's attempt to become vicariously something other than he is and his lack of self-knowledge appear literally and through symbolic detail. On the night of Jimmy's pathetic mimicry of his victorious companions, Dublin itself mimics more triumphant cities: "That night the city wore the mask of a capital" (p. 46). And as the young men approach the rowboat which will take them to the anchored yacht, Joyce describes the harbor lying "like a dark-ened mirror at their feet" (p. 47), which suggests Jimmy's (and Dublin's) lack of self-perception. The symbolic actions in the final paragraph tie up with earlier elements in the story and bring it to a significant conclusion: "He knew that he would regret in the morning but at present he was glad of the rest, glad of the dark stupor that would cover up his folly. He leaned his elbows on the table and rested his head between his hands, counting the beats of his temples. The cabin door opened and he saw the Hungarian standing in a shaft of grey light: —Daybreak, gentlemen!" (p. 48). Like the boy in "Araby," Jimmy Doyle realizes his "folly," but wishes to cover it up—he achieves a reluctant insight. He lives in his imagination; he cannot live in reality. Therefore, although earlier he had felt in his journey in the auto that he had "laid a magical finger on the genuine pulse of life," he must return at last to feeling the pulse in his own temples. Life for Jimmy remains in his head. He has intellectualized life (symbolized by the pulse); he has manufactured it out of the experience of others. Consequently he cannot be "genuinely happy," like his friends who achieve the reality of triumph.

The second symbolic action, Villona's opening of the cabin door to admit a "shaft of light," occurs in a light-darkness-light movement which is part of the first of three image patterns in the story: one according to time, another according to change of place, and, underlying these, the emotional movement within Jimmy. Of these, the first two are literally and symbolically related to the third.

In its time sequence, the story begins in the afternoon with the entry of racing cars into the city, and ends at daybreak the following morning on the yacht. One aspect of this movement from light through darkness to light again, is the "darkened mirror" image suggesting Jimmy's deficient self-knowledge. The image occurs when Jimmy is still fooling himself about the excitement of being with foreigners, and the possibility of benefitting from his association with them. Later he realizes their pursuits are not for him, for he doesn't even enjoy cards. Though he lacks the courage to request it, he wishes they would stop playing. He ends up having lost money to them, just as he has lost himself to them. The change in Jimmy from self-deception to a limited self-knowledge is implicit in his realization of "folly," a realization he happily suppresses and is imaged by the movement from night to daybreak, indicated by Villona's remark at the end of the story: "Daybreak, gentlemen!" (p. 48). Jimmy welcomes the "darkness" which would cover up his folly, just as the youth in "Araby" became aware of his vanity in seeking to re-enter the past, symbolized by the rapidly darkening hall.

Of the geographic sequence in "After the Race," Brewster Ghiselin writes: "the sweep of movement is greater than in any other story. It begins west of Dublin and ends in Kingstown Harbor."[1] The speeding cars, the rapid scene-change from the streets to Jimmy's home to the dinner downtown, and the tram-ride after which they meet the American, produce a sense of exhilarating activity. But the story ends on a yacht anchored in the harbor—an apt image for stasis.

The emotional movement parallels the imagery from a beginning of excitement, hilarity, and anticipation, to an end of disillusion, stupor, and despair. In the car, elated by rapid motion, Jimmy thinks the journey has "laid a magical finger on the genuine pulse of life" (p. 45). At the end he is on the anchored ship, taking the pulse of life in wine-benumbed temples. The rapid movement and exhilaration are associated with bohemian license, as with Eveline whom Frank takes to see "The Bohemian Girl." Despite their inclinations for licentious activity, as Ghiselin observes, both Jimmy and Eveline end in stasis.[2]

Mr. Ghiselin makes perhaps too much of the direction of geographic movement in "After the Race," noting that it goes from west to east, i.e., from the west of Dublin to the city and then to Kingstown Harbor. He implies that the west would symbolize death while, as a source of light the east would symbolize life.[3] The Christian association of the east with resurrection is clear, since Christians expect from the east the second coming of Christ, for which reason Christian burial traditionally faces the east. In the antiphons for Advent in the Roman Breviary Christ is "the Orient from on high" and "the day-star." If the movement of the story is from west to east, and the emotional movement is from hope to despair, it seems (assuming for the moment that he means any-

---

[1] Brewster Ghiselin, "The Unity of Joyce's *Dubliners*," *Accent* 16 (Summer, 1956): 200.

[2] *Ibid.*

[3] "Pride [one of the seven deadly sins] comes out of the west, the direction contrary to the vital east." *Ibid.* Mr. Ghiselin clearly stretches his point here, for one hardly sees Dublin as a center of pride. What might appear as "pride" surely is a kind of neurotic defensiveness.

thing by this directional movement) that Joyce here suggests the theme of the failure of Christianity which occurs elsewhere in *Dubliners*, as in "The Sisters" and "Eveline." More likely, however, this movement towards the east fits in with the preoccupation in *Dubliners*, and in other fiction of Joyce with the east as a source of exotic life. For example in each of the first three stories the orient forms an appropriate contrast to the tedious piety of Dublin.

Like Jimmy Doyle, Lenehan in "Two Gallants" looks for pleasure by vicarious involvement in pursuits from which he feels barred. However, in "Two Gallants" the satisfactions lack the relative gentility of those in "After the Race." More boldly than in the other stories, Joyce unveils the quest for a sexual bohemia beneath the pious sublimation of Dublin. Lenehan is the more openly homosexual of the two gallants who roam Dublin streets, preoccupied with unconventional sex.

The story details Lenehan's feeling himself into Corley's successful attempt to satisfy sexually a Dublin slavey, possibly by oral means, and to be paid by her for his achievement. Lenehan's involvement in this quest comes through his anxious imagination, by a ritual mobility, and by a symbolic meal, eaten at about the same time when Corley is "eating" the slavey. Thus bluntly outlined, the "plot" of "Two Gallants" represents a more overt expression of the wish for exotic sexuality latent in the earlier stories: implied by the dream of the protagonist of "The Sisters," of a land where the customs were strange; by the wish of the boy in "An Encounter" for "wild sensations." One recalls the buried sexual quest of Maria in "Clay," which appeared through oral imagery —barmbrack, plumcake; and of Eveline, who tentatively considered the life of a boehmian girl. These forms of sexuality have a surrogate character which implies the flight from actual sexual involvement. This flight is implicit in most of the stories, but especially in "Two Gallants," where Lenehan's flight from women appears in his conversion of sexual desire into a mode of substitution typical of the sadomasochistic character, which invariably requires, said Stekel, "flight away from the demands of the impulse into an illness."[4]

"Two Gallants" begins shortly after Corley had broached his plan to the admiring Lenehan, who shows an obscene amusement in "jets of wheezing laughter" (p. 49). His first remarks elucidate Corley's forthcoming adventure. "—Well . . . That takes the biscuit . . . . That takes the solitary, unique, and, if I may so call it, *recherché* biscuit!" (p. 50). Lenehan's experience with a woman must occur through the medium of a homosexual liaison with Corley, and by means of a symbolic communion with his friend's eccentric sexuality. His own experience is entirely surrogate and in consequence his talk about it chiefly symbolic. "Biscuit" is thus a symbol for the female genitals, especially when imagined as an object for oral gratification. Corley's anticipation is far from symbolic. In response to Lenehan's question, "Where did you pick her up?" (p. 50), Corley runs his tongue "swiftly along his upper lip" (p. 50), an action he repeats just before meeting the girl (p. 53).

Whatever psychological or social implications it may have, the precise physical object of Corley's quest is "to take the biscuit"; that is, to succeed in pleasing the girl and to be paid for his success: to "take the biscuit" in the form of the "small gold coin" which shines in his palm at the end of the story. Lenehan's anxiety on this point stems in part from a combination of fear and doubt about his own sexual prowess. He compares poorly alongside the phallic Corley, with his erect carriage and his large head, "globular and oily" that "sweated in all weathers" (p. 51).

This story ran afoul the printer's objections. The symbolic treatment of sexual subjects possibly resulted from a tactical reticence on Joyce's part not found, for example, in *Ulysses*. But, as D. H. Lawrence noted, for lack of an adequate literal vocabulary of sex in English, even in back alleys sex is discussed largely in figurative language. Thus, it would certainly be in character for Corley and Lenehan to discuss oral sexuality in symbolic terms.

[4] Wilhelm Stekel, *Sadism and Masochism: The Psychology of Hatred and Cruelty* (New York, 1963), vol. 1, p. 140.

Symbiotic with Corley, Lenehan worries that he cannot succeed with the girl. Also, he fears his friend will fail in another of his own goals—closely allied with the sexual—to get money from women: "He might yet be able to settle down in some snug corner and live happily if he could only come across some good simple-minded girl with a little of the ready" (p. 58). With gross self-assurance, Corley little doubts success, for all Lenehan's skepticism, especially about the sexual goal: "—Well . . . tell me, Corley, I suppose you'll be able to pull it off all right, eh? Corley closed one eye expressively as an answer. —Is she game for that? asked Lenehan dubiously. You can never know women. —She's all right, said Corley. I know the way to get around her, man. She's a bit gone on me. —You're what I call a gay Lothario, said Lenehan. And the proper kind of a Lothario, too!" (p. 52).

Certainly, Corley is a "gay" Lothario in the sense of a "homosexual Don Juan," by which the context defines him. With obscene suggestiveness Lenehan continues his annoying doubtfulness of his friend: "—But tell me . . . are you sure you can bring it off all right? You know it's a ticklish job. They're damn close on that point. Eh? . . . What?" (p. 53). Corley reassures him that he can succeed: "—I'll pull it off . . . Leave it to me, can't you?" (p. 53).[5]

When they encounter the slavey, Corley shows an awareness of Lenehan's peculiar enthusiasm about his own erotic life. On seeing the girl from a short distance, Lenehan, whose voice has been described as "winnowed of vigour," suddenly becomes "lively": and he wants to see the girl. In response, "Corley glanced sideways at his friend and an unpleasant grin appeared on his face. —Are you trying to get inside me? he asked" (p. 54). Of course, Lenehan is trying to get inside Corley by an imagined participation in his act, and homosexually as well. But quickly he assures Corley that he just wants to have a look at her," perhaps so that his voyeuristic phantasies will have substance. After all, as he remarks to Corley,

[5] In the letters to Nora at Cornell, Joyce occasionally used the expression, "to pull it off," to mean, "to bring about a sexual climax."

"I'm not going to eat her" (p. 54). The act of sexual eating he will leave to Corley. His own eating will take place safely in the food shop.

Whatever physical form it takes, the controlling wish of both Lenehan and Corley is the humiliation of a lower-class woman. This wish would be in line with another observation of Stekel's about the sadomasochistic inclination, which applies especially to to Lenehan's frantic imagination: "the paraphilliac identifies himself with his object; he feels himself into it so that he can experience both conditions: triumph and defeat, power and subjection, activity and passivity, male and female, resistance and the overcoming of it. The specific scene which he is always wanting to repeat is a drama, a fiction, in which he as the author feels with the actors, suffers and enjoys. This fiction has as its purpose to withdraw him from the real world."[6] One of the elements unifying sadism and masochism Stekel describes as "feeling into" the usually degrading experience of another person, ordinarily the object of affection. While this "feeling into" takes many forms, not always pathological (as with common empathy or compassion), in "Two Gallants" Joyce depicts Lenehan's feeling himself into the experience of Corley, which is both a gross humiliation and a sneering triumph: that is, sadistic and masochistic at once and for both of the "gallants." However, the story focuses on Lenehan, who plays the feminine role. In this role, he feels himself into the experience of the slavey, just as in the sadistic role he experiences what he imagines Corley to feel. Lenehan displays both "polar expressions of a single complex."[7] The "feminine" expression of his sadomasochistic complex is implicit in Lenehan's identification with the harp, a symbol for Ireland, perennially subject to "her master's hands" (p. 54). Just as Lenehan is controlled through his imagination by experience outside of himself; and as the "slavey" will submit to the mastery of Corley, so the harp—traditionally Ireland's symbol—"heedless

[6] Stekel, *Sadism and Masochism*, vol. 1., p. 56.
[7] *Ibid.*, p. 57.

that her coverings had fallen about her knees, seemed weary alike of the eyes of strangers and of her master's hands" (p. 54). Like the personified harp, like Ireland—the effeminate Ireland of "After the Race"—so, shortly after Corley leaves with the girl, Lenehan feels weary and dispirited, "His gaiety seemed to forsake him" (p. 56), and "the air which the harpist had played began to control his movements. His softly padded feet played the melody while his fingers swept a scale of variations idly along the railings after each group of notes" (p. 56). As sadistic voyeur in the degradation of others he is the harpist: as vicarious experiencer he is the harp, his movements controlled by a melody he plays in his imagination. A marionette who imagines the pulling of his own strings, he dances, even if with a merely mechanical vitality.

Each story in *Dubliners* explores not only individual plights but Joyce's view of the plight of Ireland in general: "After the Race" is not only the fine depiction of Jimmy Doyle, or even (though it is this) a careful dissection of the Catholic Irish *nouveau riche*. That story also reveals Ireland's image of herself in relation to "Continental accomplishments" of machine technology, social poise, as well as of the cool rapacity of the gaming table. "Two Gallants" also, as Joyce wrote to his brother, "with the Sunday crowds and the harp in Kildare Street and Lenehan—is an Irish landscape."[8] The sadomasochistic complexity of a Lenehan is thus the sadomasochism of Ireland: the "paralysis" at its center, the sickness Joyce meticulously described. Vicarious experience in another's degradation is essential to this complex, as it is in Ireland generally (in Joyce's view): so, of course, is the element of betrayal which preoccupied Joyce in his own relations with other people, in his fiction, and in his image of Ireland,

> This lovely land that always sent
> Her writers and artists to banishment

[8] Joyce to Stanislaus Joyce, 25 September 1906, *Letters*, vol. 2, p. 166.

> And in a spirit of Irish fun
> Betrayed her own leaders, one by one.[9]

Therefore, "Two Gallants" is not without a sense of incipient and actual betrayal.

Suspicion overshadows the liaison between Corley and Lenehan. Corley feels that Lenehan might be trying "to get inside" in his affair with the girl. He expresses also a matter of fact awareness of feminine promiscuity: "—There was others at her before me," he explains, "philosophically," and he asures Lenehan, "Didn't she tell me herself?" (p. 53). In a typical Joycean comment, Lenehan makes a "tragic gesture," and calls the girl a "base betrayer!" (p. 53). Later, as Lenehan waits for Corley, he begins to suspect that "perhaps Corley had seen her home by another way and given him the slip" (p. 59). The story is a tissue of suspicion, and suspicion of betrayal a common tone throughout Joyce's fiction. At times, suspicion of betrayal becomes a craving for the certain knowledge of betrayal. One recalls from *A Portrait of the Artist* Stephen's fabrication of his betrayal by Emma with a young priest, and later with Cranly, the betrayal of Gabriel Conroy in Gretta's recollection of Michael Furey, the betrayal of himself by his wife so carefully engineered by Richard Rowan in *Exiles*, and finally, of course, the betrayal of Bloom by Molly with Blazes Boylan which Bloom both suffers and enjoys throughout *Ulysses*. The fabrication of suspicion, especially about the faithfulness of women, permeates Joyce's writings. In early life says Stekel the sadomasochistic male concludes that "women are false and faithless." Discussing two different cases, he notes that in one the child observed his mother betraying his father and with another man. In the other, "a 'betrayal' was staged."[10] The compulsive need for betrayal grows out of an early conviction that one was betrayed. This conviction fosters endless

[9] Joyce, "Gas from a Burner," 1912, in *The Critical Writings of James Joyce*, ed. Richard Ellmann and Ellsworth Mason (New York, 1964), p. 243.
[10] Stekel, *Sadism and Masochism*, vol. 1, p. 127.

suspicion. Unfounded suspicion is one form of the play of imag- ination which replaces what actually happens with what one wishes to happen. Lenehan's sharing in Corley's sleazy triumph comes about through another operation of the same instinct to substitute imagination and mimicry for real experience which constitutes the real "action" of Joyce's Dublin. When he enters the lower-class restaurant, Lenehan places himself in circumstances which parallel what is going on between the absent Corley and his servant girl. Walking down Grafton Street, he finds trivial "all that was meant to charm him and did not answer the glances which invited him to be bold" (p. 56). Troubled as to "how he could pass the hours till he met Corley again," he has no interest in actual encounters with women of the street, because his satisfaction is surrogate; real sex- uality, "trivial." In flight from women, he soon discovers symbolic gratification: "He paused at last before the window of a poor- looking shop over which the words *Refreshment Bar* were printed in white letters. On the glass of the window were two flying in- scriptions: *Ginger Beer and Ginger Ale*. A cut ham was exposed on a great blue dish while near it on a plate lay a segment of very light plum-pudding. He eyed this food earnestly for some time and then, after glancing warily up and down the street, went into the shop quickly" (p. 57). Lenehan's "earnestly" eyeing the "ex- posed" cut ham and the segment of plum pudding suggests an in- clination to excremental vision which Joyce will later develop more fully in Leopold Bloom (though it was being developed al- ready in Joyce himself).[11] His meal in the shop will also have ex- cremental overtones: "The girl brought him a plate of hot grocer's peas, seasoned with pepper and vinegar, a fork and his ginger beer" (p. 57). But Joyce's emphasis seems rather on the way in which Lenehan's experience in the shop parallels that of Corley. First of

[11] Joyce's own coprophilia appears in letters to Nora. See especially, 16 De- cember 1909, Item 262, James Joyce Collection, Cornell University Library. Richard Ellmann has published part of this letter in vol. 2 of *Letters*, p. 276.

all, he enters only "after glancing warily up and down the street," a peculiar wariness for one who is just hungry. He feels out of place in the shop, probably in part because of a slight difference in social class. He is waited on by a "slatternly girl," which recalls the "slavey" with whom Corley is indulging. Lenehan's own unease manifests itself in a desire "to appear natural" before the mechanics in the shop, in whose eyes he does not seem a working man. He is of course a parasite on society, but more specifically on the special resources and real experience of his acquaintances: "most people considered Lenehan a leech" (p. 50). Finally, the focus of the story, essential parasitism, Joyce suggests in the detail that Lenehan "sipped his ginger beer and sat for some time thinking of Corley's adventure," which leads him to reflect on "his own poverty of purse and spirit"; typically this poverty he thinks of alleviating in the reflection that, "He might yet be able to settle down in some snug corner and live happily if he could only come across some good simple-minded girl with a little of the ready" (p. 58).

Also implied in "Two Gallants" is a connection between Irish sexual malaise and Germanic sexual brutality which would appear tenuous indeed were it not that Joyce indicated such a connection. In a letter to Grant Richards he wrote:

> I am sorry you do not tell me why the printer . . . refuses to print *Two Gallants* . . . Is it the small gold coin in the . . . story or the code of honour which the two gallants live by which shocks him? I see nothing which should shock him in either of these things. His idea of gallantry has grown up in him (probably) during the reading of the novels of the elder Dumas and during the performance of romantic plays which presented to him cavaliers and ladies in full dress. But I am sure he is willing to modify his fantastic views. I would strongly recommend to him the chapters wherein Ferrero examines the moral code of the soldier and (incidentally) of the gallant. But it would be useless for I am sure that in his heart of hearts he is a militarist.[12]

[12] Joyce to Grant Richards, 5 May 1906, *Letters*, vol. 2, pp. 132–133.

The importance of Ferrero's book *L'Europa giovane* for this story Joyce acknowledged also in a letter to Stanislaus in which he says Ferrero gave him the "idea" for "Two Gallants."[13] Ferrero concerns himself primarily with the psychological and social differences between Germanic and Latin peoples.[14] The Irish do not fit precisely in either category, since though at one point he says they are expansive like the French, at another he omits them from his list of Latin peoples (Italy, France, Spain) and Germanic (England, Germany, Scandinavia, Finland). More than likely, Ferrero gave little thought to the Irish. He does not include Dublin among the cities he writes about extensively—London, Paris, Moscow, Rome, Stockholm—as though to verify Joyce's own feeling that Ireland was a provincial backwater, hardly imagined a part of Europe by cosmopolitan Europeans like Ferrero. Thus, Joyce's wish to give Dublin to the world as other "capitals" had been given forms part of his achievement in rendering the peculiarly "Irish landscape" of "Two Gallants."[15] The story can be viewed as a fictional footnote to Ferrero's book, and Joyce's mood appears to have been to assign to Ireland both Germanic and Latin attributes, as far as his psychological depiction of her is concerned. Therefore, the connection between Ferrero's book and "Two Gallants," the idea Joyce got from it for his story, seems not so much in what Ferrero says about the Irish, for he says relatively little about them, but in what he says about the economic-sexual-militaristic proclivities of Germanic peoples, and the sexual-economic proclivities of the Latins. The idea in Joyce's letter to Grant Richards is that erotic militarism has been pictured by the Latin imagination as a cavalier romanticism. As Ferrero points out, in his comments on "southern love," in the south men live and fight for "love," especially for the physical

[13] Joyce to Stanislaus Joyce, 11 February 1907, *Letters*, vol. 2, p. 212.

[14] Guglielmo Ferrero, *L'Europa giovane* (Milan, 1897), p. 123.

[15] "The book is not a collection of tourist impressions but an attempt to represent certain aspects of the life of one of the European capitals." Joyce to William Heinemann, 23 September 1905, *Letters*, vol. 2, p. 109.

beauty of women.[16] But in "Two Gallants" Corley and Lenehan live to violate nature and to get money, which are Germanic goals.

The "moral code" in "Two Gallants" resembles the militarism Ferrero described in Bismarck. The soldier needs to arouse man's inert brutality, which enables him to fulfill his need to violate nature.[17] In Bismarck, this took the form of a desire to crush France, which represented to him a seductive sexuality opposed to the extremes of brutal vice and absolute virtue his teutonic temperament preferred.[18] The rewards for violent indulgence are power and money: pride and honor. Typically, the Germanic warrior fought for gold, as the Latin for love. Corley, the erect, brutal, stolid "Prussian," must violate nature with the "slavey," who, with her blunt features, "projecting front teeth," and "contented leer" (p. 56), recalls Ferrero's description of brutal Berlin prostitution (compared with seductive Parisian prostitution).[19] Corley must return from his conquest with the small coin of gold, for which, said Ferrero, the Germanic warriors of legend invariably struggled.[20]

The "Latin" aspects of Dublin are less obvious, especially since Joyce did not mention them specifically. Corley is a "gay Lothario," both a Don Giovanni and a Bismarck, a peculiarly Joycean combination which parallels the Joycean image of women as "obscene madonnas." Lenehan and Corley certainly shun one aspect of the nordic disposition, a devotion to labor and the ascetic life. Ferrero said that the Italians, for example, avoid work between the ages of fifteen and twenty-five because they are taken up with sex.[21] Joyce's "gallants" are both, of course, parasites. Especially Lenehan wishes for a woman "with a little of the ready," not so much because cash represents conquest to him, as it might to a Germanic type, but

---

[16] Ferrero, *L'Europa giovane*, p. 141.
[17] *Ibid.*, pp. 31, 32.
[18] *Ibid.*, p. 164.
[19] *Ibid.*, pp. 165, 166.
[20] *Ibid.*, pp. 136, 139.
[21] *Ibid.*, p. 127.

because he prefers indulgence and despises work which, in Ferrero's terms, would attribute to him Latin rather than Germanic characteristics.

Therefore, the "gallantry" in "Two Gallants" is neither that of the Latin cavalier exclusively nor that alone of the Bismarckian brute, but a typically Irish game played against the tedious backdrop of an Irish landscape, "shuttered for the repose of Sunday" (p. 49), echoing with a wheezing laughter. The experience of Joyce's Ireland includes Latin and Germanic vices as it excludes Latin and Germanic virtues.

Concerning the unfavorable depiction of Irish femininity throughout *Dubliners*, with the emphasis in "Two Gallants" on brutal, lower-class female sexuality, one ought to comment briefly on Joyce's general attitude towards women. For example, a number of critics argue that in *Ulysses*, Joyce deifies women in Molly Bloom, who becomes for W. Y. Tindall a substitution for the Virgin,[22] for Stuart Gilbert the "Great Mother" goddess whom the Romans invoked,[23] and for Harry Levin an incarnation of "the fertility of the earth."[24] But, Edwin R. Steinberg maintains that Molly is "completely egocentric . . . snobbish and self-confident . . . sensual . . . ignorant, inconsistent, and superficial, etc."[25] She is the antithesis of "twentieth century earth goddess,"[26] and certainly not inconsistent with the idea that the Joycean attitude toward women, in his work, is frequently contemptuous. J. Mitchell Morse makes many of these same points: he also opposes the "cliché" of Molly as an "earth goddess," etc. He writes, "Molly is not honest, she is not kind, she is not creative, she is not free, she hasn't enough *élan vital* to get dressed before three p.m., and her fertility is subnor-

[22] W. Y. Tindall, *James Joyce* (New York, 1950), p. 37.

[23] Stuart Gilbert, *James Joyce's "Ulysses"* (New York, 1952), p. 32.

[24] Harry Levin, *James Joyce: A Critical Introduction* (Norfolk, 1941), p. 125.

[25] Edwin R. Steinberg, "A Book with A Molly in It," *James Joyce Review* 2, nos. 1 and 2 (June, 1958): 61.

[26] *Ibid.*, p. 58.

mal."[27] As with many critical appraisals of Joyce's work, these views are too one-sided. Joyce's true attitude can only be described as ambiguous: Molly is *both* earth-mother and infertile, goddess and bitch. The slavey in "Two Gallants" is a combination of pig and Nausicaa wearing sailor's clothing: "She had broad nostrils, a straggling mouth which lay open in a contented leer, and two projecting front teeth" (p. 56). Stanislaus Joyce remarked in *My Brother's Keeper* that "my brother, I am afraid, never quite rid himself of that Iago complex toward women, *radix malorum*, which he imbibed in youth."[28] Joyce had considerable reservations about intellectual woman, which helps to account for his attraction to Nora. Joyce's picture of the slavey in "Two Gallants" could be derived from Nora, herself a "slavey."

Little Chandler and Ignatius Gallaher of "A Little Cloud" resemble the two gallants in that both pairs are made up of a Don Juan and the less assertive male protagonist.[29] Corley speaks freely of his sexual conquests to Lenehan; Ignatius Gallaher boasts of his experience in a world alien to his envious and timid friend. Lenehan ignores the women they pass in the street; Little Chandler passes women "without turning his head to look" (p. 72). For all of his "detachment," Lenehan vicariously takes part in his partner's achievement. Despite agoraphobic timidity, Little Chandler ambivalently courts what he fears. He wishes to be seduced, and yet "at times a sound of low fugitive laughter made him tremble like a leaf" (p. 72). He resembles the boy in "The Sisters" whom the work of "paralysis" both attracted and terrified.

---

[27] J. Mitchell Morse, "Molly Bloom Revisited," *A James Joyce Miscellany,* 2nd Series, ed. Marvin Magalaner (Carbondale, 1959), pp. 139–140.

[28] Stanislaus Joyce, *My Brother's Keeper* (New York, 1958), p. 254.

[29] Aggressive Corley and reticent Lenehan, Ignatius Gallaher and Little Chandler, are paralleled by a series of male pairs in *Dubliners, A Portrait of the Artist* (Stephen and Cranly), *Ulysses* (Stephen and Mulligan), and *Finnegans Wake* (Shem and Shaun). These parallels Julian B. Kaye has noted, especially the contrast between an aggressive Maloney and the uncertain narrator in "An Encounter." "The Wings of Daedalus: Two Stories in *Dubliners,*" *Modern Fiction Studies* 4 (Spring, 1958): 35.

Little Chandler, a diminutive law clerk, hastens to a reunion in Corless's Pub with Ignatius Gallaher, an old acquaintance lately returned from newspaper work on the continent, who boasts of his experience and knowledge, particularly of continental sexual behavior. Envying Gallaher's freedom, Little Chandler becomes freshly aware of his own dreary life in Dublin, particularly the frustration of his poetic aspirations. He returns home to a shrewish wife, who snaps at him furiously when after stepping out briefly she discovers their infant, left in its father's care, crying because of a sudden outburst of annoyance from Little Chandler.[30]

Stressing the physical diminutiveness of Little Chandler, Joyce implies both psychological and sexual immaturity.[31] In addition to the title, one cannot miss the repetition of "little" throughout the story in descriptions of the principal character. Along with reference to his childish dimensions Little Chandler's sexual inadequacy shows throughout his conversation with Ignatius Gallaher, and through hints such as that Little Chandler's wife is the prisoner of her husband's sexual inadequacy—her photograph enclosed in "a frame of crumpled horn" (p. 82), a description which, thus interpreted, might account for the intensity of Annie's gruff behavior. Closely connected with the imagery of diminution is that of imprisonment. His own neurotic inadequacy imprisons both Little Chandler and his wife. Their liaison foreshadows Leopold and Molly Bloom. Though he is imprisoned by Dublin itself, the barriers which inhibit Little Chandler's growth are also internal. From his point of view, he is chiefly a prisoner of environment, a

[30] Mark Schorer has suggested the structural order in this story by questioning the emotional state of Little Chandler before, during, and after the encounter with his old friend. Mark Schorer, ed., *The Story: A Critical Anthology* (New York, 1950), pp. 288–305.

[31] Magalaner notes the emphasis on diminutiveness. Concerning this it is significant that Maria, in "Clay," is also described in such a way that her diminutiveness is emphasized. In both stories Joyce conveys through this imagery the concept of personalities which are stunted, especially in respect to their sexual development. "James Joyce's *Dubliners*," Ph.D. dissertation (New York, 1951), p. 143.

self-deception to which the smallness of his character should dispose him.

Related to the depiction of Little Chandler's self-imprisonment and his stunted character, is the imagery from Byron's poem, "On the Death of a Young Lady."[32] "Within this narrow cell reclines her clay, That clay where once . . ." (p. 84). The idea throughout the story has been of Little Chandler's imprisonment ("He was a prisoner for life," etc., p. 84). Here, however, he reads a poem referring to a *woman* who is in her grave, which is likened to a "cell." The imprisonment of death is like Little Chandler's living imprisonment—but, since the earlier part of the verse reads,

> Hushed are the winds and still the evening gloom,
> Not e'en a Zephyr wanders through the grove,
> Whilst I return to view my Margaret's tomb
> And scatter flowers on the dust I love. (p. 85)

Joyce may be implying that Little Chandler's gentle melancholy attaches to a dead person; his imprisonment in life stems from his masochistic imprisonment in death, in the "narrow cell" of her tomb. Still a child (even his teeth are "childish"), he cannot grow because he is still involved with the dead. His past has imprisoned him and his escape into Byron recalls an earlier enclosure because of which, as for all the Dubliners, the present brings unsurpassable limitations.

As with Lenehan and Corley, there is a homosexual affinity between Little Chandler and Ignatius Gallaher, with Little Chandler in the feminine role: "His hands were white and small, his frame was fragile, his voice was quiet and his manners were refined. He took the greatest care of his fair silken hair and moustache and used perfume discreetly on his handkerchief" (p. 70). He fears not only

---

[32] Clarice Short has drawn out in detail the idea that Little Chandler is to be thought of as a prisoner. She points out the many similarities between Joyce's Little Chandler and Byron's Prisoner of Chillon. "Joyce's 'A Little Cloud,' " *MLN* 72 (1957): 275–278.

his wife, but women he passes in the street as with pleasant terror and "walking swiftly by at night" he passed Corless's and saw the richly dressed ladies who "caught up their dresses, when they touched earth, like alarmed Atalantas" (p. 72). Comically, he inflates them to the image of Atalanta, the athletic goddess suckled by a she-bear, finally turned into a lioness for her profanation of Aphrodite's shrine. Though it were best not to court the alarm of Atalantan women, he does in time alarm his wife, Atalantan on a domestic scale.

Ignatius Gallaher suggests to his bewildered friend visions of exotic sexuality not found in the middle-class Dublin bedroom. These suggestions have homosexual overtones. His interrogation of Little Chandler soon gets down to specifics: "Have you never been anywhere, even for a trip? —I've been to the Isle of Man, said Little Chandler. Ignatius Gallaher laughed. —The Isle of Man! he said. Go to London or Paris: Paris, for choice. That'd do you good" (p. 76). Though "the Isle of Man" has homosexual implications, it is also a typical choice of Little Chandler's sexual timidity. Ignatius Gallaher recommends the bohemianism of Paris: "I've been to all the Bohemian cafes. Hot stuff! Not for a pious chap like you, Tommy" (p. 76). The conversation proceeds to suggestions of oral sexuality reminiscent of "Two Gallants" and implied throughout *Dubliners*: "—Everything in Paris is gay, said Ignatius Gallaher. They believe in enjoying life—and don't you think they're right? If you want to enjoy yourself properly you must go to Paris. And, mind you, they've a great feeling for the Irish there. When they heard I was from Ireland they were ready to eat me, man" (p. 77).

Responding to Little Chandler's "timid insistence," Ignatius Gallaher, "in a calm historian's tone," outlines "some pictures of the corruption which was rife abroad" (p. 78), in contrast with "old jog-along Dublin where nothing is known of such things" (p. 78). At this Little Chandler is astonished, then quickly humiliated when his coarse interrogator starts to pry into his marriage. Three small whiskies, Gallaher's suspicious history, the light and noise of Corless's, "upset the equipoise of his sensitive nature" (p. 80); they combine to jolt loose the repressed desires indicated by his constant "blushing." Duped by Gallaher, he feels that his "unfortunate timidity" had stood in the way of his doing even better than his friend: "He wished to vindicate himself in some way, to assert his manhood" (p. 80). His assertion takes the form of predicting the marriage of Gallaher, which soon also gets on to sexual specifics: the notion of marriage as a sexual condescension: "—No blooming fear of that, my boy. I'm going to have my fling first and see a bit of life and the world before I put my head in the sack—if I ever do. —Some day you will, said Little Chandler calmly" (p. 81). In self-defense, Ignatius Gallaher turns full upon his friend: "—You think so? he said. —You'll put your head in the sack, repeated Little Chandler stoutly, like everyone else if you can find the girl" (p. 81). Immediately, Little Chandler blushes again, aware of having "betrayed himself." But reminiscent of "Two Gallants," his friend insists that if he marries, "she'll have a good fat account at the bank or she won't do for me" (p. 81). This final shot reaffirms Gallaher's reluctance to condescend to the bondage of Dublin marriage, especially its oral-sexual aspect: "—But I'm in no hurry . . . I don't fancy tying myself up to one woman, you know. He imitated with his mouth the act of tasting and made a wry face. —Must get a bit stale, I should think, he said" (p. 82).

Ignatius Gallaher exerts a power over his diminutive friend because he sees into the compromise with his desires which marriage has afforded Little Chandler; their meeting centers around Little Chandler's gradually more embarrassing awareness that he has been found out. His inclinations are homosexual, but he has compromised them in marriage.

Later, in *Ulysses*, Joyce will be more explicit about a similar compromise in the character of Leopold Bloom—like Little Chandler, a bit of a poet, like him, with his "head in the sack." In *Ulysses*, the "wry face" is made by Molly, in recollection of Bloom's oral indulgence on returning to the accommodating bed in Eccles

Street, where his day ends "with obscure prolonged provocative melon smellonous osculation" of Molly's rump (p. 719.) In her interior monologue, Molly thinks: "Any man that'd kiss a woman's bottom I'd throw my hat at him after that he'd kiss anything unnatural . . . before I ever do that to a man pfooh the filthy brutes the mere thought is enough" (p. 762).

Little Chandler's return home, after his visit with Gallaher, has a different emphasis. While holding the baby for his wife, he falls into daydreams contrasting the cold eyes of his wife's photograph with those of the "rich Jewesses" Gallaher had mentioned: "Those dark Oriental eyes, he thought, how full they are of passion, of voluptuous longing! . . . Why had he married the eyes in the photograph?" (p. 83). He goes on to imagine a career as poet and he begins to read from Byron. But the domestic compromise begins to force him back into repression. The baby awakens, wails. Little Chandler yells furiously for it to stop. His wife returns and, at the end, he sustains briefly "the gaze of her eyes and his heart closed together as he met the hatred in them" (p. 85). The closing of his heart is a typical image for the neurotic acquiesence of Dublin.

In "Counterparts," as in "A Little Cloud," an unhappy husband briefly escapes everyday tedium in the illusory freedom of Dublin pubs where feelings of frustration and inferiority balloon. Back home, these feelings are taken out on helpless children. In both stories, the buildup and release of emotion does not issue in liberation but in futility: we are more conscious of bondage at the end than we were before.

A sullen clerk, the gigantic Farrington responds with a flippant remark to the senile tyranny of his boss, Mr. Alleyne. This petty triumph he repeats among his parasitic cronies in the pubs. But his feelings are short-lived. He is made to apologize abjectly to Mr. Alleyne; his cronies drink him penniless; an English girl snubs him, a puny Englishman defeats him in Indian wrestling. Smouldering, he goes home and beats his small son for having let the fire die.

His resentment for Mr. Alleyne derives not only from his subordinate role, but from his envious perception of the liaison between his boss and a Miss Delacour. Just before his provocative remark, he glances from her face to that of his boss and back again. His witticism provokes her broad smile. He ingratiates himself with her by diminishing her regard for Mr. Alleyne, who trembles afterwards with "a dwarf's passion." Alleyne is a Humpty Dumpty figure, whose head "seemed like a large egg reposing on the papers" (p. 87).[33] Farrington stares "at the polished skull . . . gauging its fragility" (p. 87). His tongue finds "a felicitous moment" as he glances again at "the little egg-shaped head" (p. 91). Excusing his work by reference to the chief clerk, Farrington strikes a venal blow for liberty, by association with Shelley, who exhorted the overthrow of tyranny. This in spite of his boss: "Kindly attend to what I say and not to what *Mr. Shelley says sir.* You have always some excuse or another for shirking work" (p. 87).

Though in "A Little Cloud," Joyce emphasized the diminutiveness of Little Chandler, he stresses the physical gigantism of Farrington, who "was tall and of great bulk" (p. 86). Farrington is strong and inclined to violence: "He felt strong enough to clear out the whole office single-handed. His body ached to do something, to rush out and revel in violence" (p. 90). And yet, though outwardly the opposite of Little Chandler, he struggles inwardly with the notion of his own smallness, which he projects on others, whose smallness preoccupies him.

In three contests of "strength," Farrington engages with others smaller than himself. References to Mr. Alleyne's dwarfishness

[33] Humpty Dumpty as a symbol for the fragile authority, Joyce will extend later. Mr. Alleyne's "fall" is a prefiguration of the fall of Humpty Dumpty in *Finnegans Wake*, as recounted in "The Ballad of Persse O'Reilly." It is that also of authorities in several domains: God, the "fafafather of all schemes for to bother us"; Cromwell, "Lord Olofa Crumple," in the political order; St. Thomas Aquinas, "the old hayheaded philosopher" (on his deathbed St. Thomas is said to have regarded all of his writings as "straw"); and, of course, Earwicker, who is the fallen authority in the familial sphere. The ballad also contains direct or indirect reference to Thor, Noah, and Wellington, authorities of myth, the Bible, and military life. *Finnegans Wake*, pp. 44–47.

occur several times. He is a "manikin." Farrington thinks of Weathers, who defeats him at hand-wrestling, as "a stripling." Later, Joyce reminds us four times that Farrington's unfortunate son is a "little boy," or, as Farrington refers to him, "a little whelp!" (p. 98). Like Mr. Alleyne, Farrington's own passion is "a dwarf's passion," ultimately as futile as the frantic weakness of his son, who "clasped his hands together in the air and [whose] voice shook with fright" (p. 98). As with his father, as with most of Joyce's Dubliners, at the center of paralysis, he is powerless.

Stekel has said that the sadomasochist identifies with the abasement of others, partly out of revenge, partly because in the weakness of others he sees his own: also because, powerless, he gets power through vicarious experience. With delight, Farrington observed the humiliation of his boss in front of Miss Delacour because he felt it himself as, in the pub, he will feel directly humiliated by the gaudy young woman with a London accent and by the strong Englishman, Weathers. The wheel comes full circle when he again both debases and avenges himself in the cruel humiliation of little Tim, his own flesh and blood. The sadomasochism is in the surrogate character of his expressions of violence, his "feeling into" the plights of others who, in common with him, display real ineffectuality. But, relatively defenseless, they provide targets vulnerable enough for small artillery.

The title of "Counterparts" must mean that Mr. Alleyne is to Farrington as Farrington is later to his son. He takes out his violence on a weaker person because he can't do so with either his boss or with Weathers, the stronger Englishman. Therefore, Farrington parrots his son's plea for mercy: "He began to mimic his son's flat accent, saying to himself: *At the chapel. At the chapel, if you please"* (p. 97). Earlier, Mr. Alleyne had insultingly parroted Farrington's plea: "—*Mr Shelley said, sir.* . . . Kindly attend to what I say and not to what *Mr Shelley says sir*" (p. 87). Joyce sympathized with Farrington's need to play a role of power denied to him in life. Concerning "Counterparts," he wrote to Stanislaus: "I am no friend of tyranny, as you know, but if many husbands are brutal the atmosphere in which they live is brutal and few wives and homes can satisfy the desire for happiness."[34]

This statement suggests that Joyce preferred a naturalistic explanation for the story: Farrington as a victim of pressure of environment. But Farrington is also portrayed as setting himself up for brutal treatment by mocking the Northern Irish accent of Mr. Alleyne—who represents the Anglo-Irish ascendency. He will provoke an even more vehement wrath with his spontaneous reply to Alleyne's question. "Tell me . . . do you take me for a fool? Do you think me an utter fool? (p. 91). Farrington answers, "—I don't think, sir . . . that that's a fair question to put to me" (p. 91). Immediately, his acid response evokes "a dwarf's passion," which, in its very dwarfishness, resembles that of little Tom in the end. Thus, one may explain the title of the story not only in the obvious sense— as Mr. Alleyne tyrannizes Farrington, so Farrington torments his helpless son; but also in the sense that as Farrington torments his "manikin" boss, so he later torments his small son. He resembles the shrewd cronies in "A Mother," who are ostensibly the prey of a tyrannical Mrs. Kearney, but who both provoke their own victimization and victimize their own tormentor. As usual with Joyce's Dubliners, Farrington's behavior is sadistic and masochistic at one and the same time.[35]

[34] Joyce to Stanislaus Joyce, 13 November 1906, *Letters*, vol. 2, p. 192.
[35] William B. Stein has seen a more grandiose moralism in this story. Farrington is "the embodiment of unrestrained animalism," who instead of expiating his sins surrenders to the seven deadly sins, etc. That Joyce criticizes Dubliners such as Farrington from the point of view of a Jesuit retreatmaster is difficult to accept. " 'Counterparts': A Swing Song," *James Joyce Quarterly* 1, no. 2 (Winter, 1964): 30–32.

CHAPTER IV

"Ivy Day in the Committee Room" and "The Dead": Paralysis as Pretense

SPIRITUAL PARASITISM is a central experience of Joyce's Dubliners. Unable to live satisfactorily for themselves, they feed on the real or imagined strength of those they envy and despise, degrading themselves and sapping the energy of their host-victim. Sadomasochists, they defeat themselves in defeating others. In "Ivy Day in the Committee Room," the image of ineffectual politicians "laid low" by treachery to their chiefs, to each other, to themselves, occurs against the rhetoric of a poem commemorating the betrayal of Parnell, which they project on others but which they themselves have caused. Clearly, Joyce meant Hynes's poem comically to apply to the disciples in the upper room, most of whom are Judas figures: "They had their way: they laid him low."[1] The Dubliners need only put on the face of pious blankness; they pretend roles they do not truly feel: in "Ivy Day in the Committee Room," the role of political and social loyalty.

[1] Joseph L. Blotner deals at length with the circumstantial parallels of Parnell with Christ. The disciples of both speak of them after their deaths in an upper room: three of the Dubliners, Henchy, O'Connor, and Hynes, have the names of disciples. Priests conspired against both Christ and Parnell. And, finally, the poem read at the end of the story recounts episodes in Parnell's life which are analogous to those in the life of Christ. Blotner does not fail, of course, to point out a number of contrasts between Christ and Parnell: Christ rose, Parnell disappeared; Parnell left behind him a coterie of followers who were paralyzed, Christ's followers were dedicated. " 'Ivy Day in the Committee Room': Death Without Resurrection," *Perspective* 9 (Summer, 1957): 210–217.

In "The Dead," parasitism becomes spiritual vampirism. The living feed on the dead, the dead on the living. The lives of others keep Dublin alive, even in its supposedly most gratifying aspect, the hospitality which Joyce felt obliged to honor, however ambiguously. Even one of the chief literary origins of "The Dead," Ibsen's *When We Dead Awaken*, focuses on the theme of spiritual parasitism which I will examine after a look at "Ivy Day in the Committee Room."

In a letter to Stanislaus in which Joyce checks details about political practice in Dublin for "Ivy Day in the Committee Room," he wrote that he would like to write sentences "about the people who betrayed me. . . . After all, there are many ways of betraying people."[2] Betrayal was in his mind at the time he wrote "Ivy Day in the Committee Room"; his own identification with Parnell is well known. Betrayal and the constant suspicion of it was a prevalent theme in his own life and in his work and "Ivy Day in the Committee Room," so pervaded by its sense, was first in his affections.[3] But there are "many ways of betraying people," and "Ivy Day in the Committee Room" displays a number of them. The story describes the gradual accumulation in a gloomy upper room of a group of Dubliners, who have been desultorily canvassing for Mr. Tierney, candidate in a municipal election. Well-oiled by on-the-cuff stout, they discuss politics, backbite one another, and finally lapse into beery sentiment at the reading of a poem about Parnell.

Betrayal usually requires a pose of loyalty. The fire, "a whitening dome of coals," serves as stage lighting. It subtly reveals both role and reality, at the end associated with "the monarch's pyre" of Parnell, on which Erin's hopes and dreams "perish," but from which

[2] Joyce to Stanislaus Joyce, about 24 September 1905, *Letters*, vol. 2, ed. Richard Ellmann (New York, 1966), p. 110.

[3] Joyce wrote that "Two Gallants," *after* "Ivy Day in the Committee Room," was the story which "pleases me most." Joyce to Grant Richards, 20 May 1906, *Letters*, ed. Stuart Gilbert (New York, 1966), vol. 1, p. 62. This opinion, of course, precedes the inclusion of "The Dead" in *Dubliners*.

the Phoenix, Parnell's spirit, may rise again.[4] As revealing agent, the fire also provides the only adequate commentary on the sentimental posing of Hynes's auditors, by the laconically irreverent bottle of stout which has been warming in the fire: "*Pok!* The cork flew out of Mr Hynes's bottle, but Mr Hynes remained sitting, flushed and bareheaded on the table. He did not seem to have heard the invitation" (p. 135).

The fire is a rhetorical device of evaluation much as the wind both comments on and expresses the bombastic illusion of Dublin enthymeme in the *Aeolus* episode of *Ulysses*. Speaking through the true source of Dublin "spirituality," a bottle of stout, the fire's "pok" discloses by comic diminution that Dublin's true Phoenix is really a beery flatulence.

The first sentences constitute stage directions: "Old Jack raked the cinders together with a piece of cardboard and spread them judiciously over the whitening dome of coals. When the dome was thinly covered his face lapsed into darkness but, as he set himself to fan the fire again, his crouching shadow ascended the opposite wall and his face slowly re-emerged into light. It was an old man's face, very bony and hairy. The moist blue eyes blinked at the fire and the moist mouth fell open at times, munching once or twice mechanically when it closed" (p. 118). The fire is like stage lighting, rheostatically controlled as carefully as Joyce's prose. Really in the dark, then "a crouching shadow," then "munching mechanically," Old Jack plays the role of devoted father, in the act of slandering his "boosing" son: "I tried to make him someway decent. . . . —Only I'm an old man now I'd change his tune for him. I'd take the stick to his back and beat him while I could stand over him—as I done many a time before" (pp. 119–120).

A counterfeit of power, he speaks to O'Connor whose own voice is a "husky falsetto." O'Connor is supposed to be canvassing for

---

[4] The fire is an image for "the flame of life, dying in dying Dublin in spite of care." W. Y. Tindall, *A Reader's Guide to James Joyce* (New York, 1959), p. 35.

Mr. Tierney, "but, as the weather was inclement . . . he spent a great part of the day sitting by the fire in the Committee Room" (p. 119). His false devotion to Mr. Tierney appears in his lighting a cigaret with the strip of pasteboard card advertising his employer—the implication being that Mr. Tierney's hopes will perish as Parnell's did in the funeral pyre of Ireland's petty treachery. This implication strengthens when O'Connor's burning pasteboard "lit up a leaf of dark glossy ivy in the lapel of his coat" (p. 119). The ivy is Parnell's symbol as October sixth is his day.

Mr. Hynes, the devoted follower of Parnell, enters to insist on light and comment on Old Jack's preference for darkness: "—What are you doing in the dark? he asks. —Is that you, Hynes? asked Mr. O'Connor. —Yes. What are you doing in the dark?" (p. 120). In response, the old man lights candlesticks in the fire, an act which introduces a complex and enlightening discussion of Dublin politics, its object to see the light of shoddy motivation which passes both for power and loyalty in Dublin. The discussion continues intermittently among the room's comings and goings until Hynes's poem is read; it illuminates not only Dublin politicians but their hacks as well.

Hynes suspects "Tricky Dicky" Tierney of seeking office for his own advantage: "This fellow you're working for only wants to get some job or other," as opposed to Colgan, "a plain honest man . . . [who] goes in to represent the labour classes" (p. 121). Those who canvass for Tierney are like him, chiefly interested in their own advantage, their "spondulics"; when Mr. Henchy enters, his first words are, "—No money, boys" (p. 122). Again, for his own advantage, "fat jobs for his sons and nephews and cousins" (p. 121), Tierney advocates presenting an address of welcome on King Edward's forthcoming visit. By contrast, this would remind Hynes's hearers of Parnell's explicit prohibition to his followers, as Joyce wrote in a news article on Parnell, against receiving "officially any member of the British royal house until the English government should restore autonomy to Ireland."[5] Mr. Hynes refers to the prohibition when, pointing to the ivy leaf in his lapel, he says: "—If this man was alive . . . we'd have no talk of an address of welcome" (p. 122).

If Hynes represents unalloyed devotion to Parnell and well-grounded suspicion of the nouveau politicians, like Tierney, who have replaced Parnell, Mr. Henchy stands for the paranoid suspicion and masochistic hatred which blights the hopes of Ireland. The conflict in this story consists of the opposition between both spirits. The antagonism between Hynes and Henchy shows in Henchy's nodding "curtly" to Hynes, who soon leaves. Mr. Henchy waits a few moments for Hynes to be off before launching a comic character assassination: "—To tell you my private and candid opinion, he said, I think he's a man from the other camp. He's a spy of Colgan's if you ask me" (p. 124). Gradually, his fear that "our friend is not nineteen karat" almost includes the suspicion that "he is in the pay of the castle," though, having planted the suspicion in his hearers, he skillfully adds: "No, damn it, I think he's a stroke above that" (p. 125).

In the midst of this detraction enters Dublin clerical life in the form of Father Keon, the "unfortunate" priest, resembling "a poor clergyman or a poor actor" (p. 125). He is a figure of "mystery," as Henchy says, "an unfortunate man of some kind." In the published version of the story, Joyce only suggests that Father Keon's misfortune had to do with perversity: he speaks with a "discreet, indulgent, velvety voice." In the manuscript Joyce was more explicit, adding to the above description (but later crossing it out), "which is not often found except with the confessor or the sodomite."[6]

---

[5] "The Shade of Parnell" in *The Critical Writings of James Joyce,* ed. Richard Ellmann and Ellsworth Mason (New York, 1964), p. 227.

[6] This handwritten manuscript I found with Item 30 in the Joyce Collection at the Cornell University Library. It is not described in Robert Scholes's catalogue, *The Cornell Joyce Collection* (Ithaca, 1961), because it was acquired later. See Scholes, "Further Observations on the Text of *Dubliners,*" *Studies*

Father Keon recalls Father Flynn of "The Sisters," whose sexual perversity Joyce suggested and who was also an unsuccessful priest.

His abrupt entrance in "Ivy Day in the Committee Room" is difficult to account for. He is one of those puzzling eccentrics who often appear in Joyce's fiction, without apparent reason, like the old sodomite in "An Encounter"; or the old sailor in the Eumaeus episode of *Ulysses*. They inhabit insane worlds which usually parody what passes for sanity in Dublin. At first glance one cannot tell whether Father Keon is "a poor clergyman or a poor actor." It is not even possible to say "whether he wore a clergyman's collar or a layman's," (p. 125). His face is that of a decadent clown with the appearance of "damp yellow cheese save where two rosy spots indicated the cheekbones" (p. 125).

After Father Keon leaves, Mr. O'Connor asks Henchy, "—What is he exactly?" Henchy, who generally pretends knowledge, replies, "—Ask me an easier one" (p. 126). They find him mysterious because he mirrors their own disposition, about which, like Old Jack, they are "in the dark." The intrusion of Father Keon as mirror figure Joyce implies in the situation itself. Father Keon is either an actor or a priest, but neither clearly, just as the shabby hacks in the committee room are playing the interrelated roles of political canvassers for Tierney (a parody of Parnell), and devoted wearers of Parnell's ivy. As Father Keon failed in his priestly allegiance, they fail in their political loyalties. They act out of opportunism as, in Henchy's explanation of how the priest "knocks it out" (p. 126), Father Keon travels on "his own account." They travel also on their "own accounts" as economic parasites, with no fixed attachments, but with inclinations for accruing petty debts. On credit Mr. Henchy ordered the dozen stout which they begin to drink after a discussion in which, foreshadowing Bloom in the "Circe" episode, Henchy, Old Jack, and O'Connor play the comic roles of Lord

in Bibliography 17 (1964): 121. I am indebted to Professor George Healey, curator of rare books at Cornell University for permission to examine the Joyce material.

Mayor, his attendant, and his private secretary respectively: "—Driving out of the Mansion House, said Mr. Henchy, in all my vermin, with Jack here standing up behind me in a powdered wig,—eh!" (p. 127). Henchy's deliberate "vermin" for "ermine" surely implies the parasitic threat all three are for the public life in Dublin. Their similarity with Father Keon—the ambiguous actor-priest—shows in their inclusion of him in the act. As Henchy says: "I'll make Father Keon my private chaplain. We'll have a family party" (p. 127). They are brothers in the parasitic buffoonery of Dublin politics. Their concept of public power as basically an act played before the world shows in the disparaging criticism of the Lord Mayor's thrift. Jack says to Henchy: "Faith, Mr Henchy . . . you'd keep up better style than some of them" (pp. 127–128). The buffoonery culminates in the recitation of Hynes's poem, which deplores the betrayal of Parnell. Mr. Henchy, who has opportunistically advocated the reception of King Edward in Ireland—a betrayal of Parnell's ghost —poses as a grateful recipient of the poetic tribute to Parnell: "—What did you think of that, Crofton? cried Mr Henchy. Isn't that fine? What?" (p. 135). With aloof irony Crofton, not a Parnellite, provides the final lines in this story. Joyce slyly notes that "Mr Crofton said that it was a very fine piece of writing" (p. 135).

Although for certain critics it ends on a hopeful note, in my view "The Dead" ends more conclusively than any of the stories in a mood of softly falling desperation.[7] As with his younger counter-

[7] Kenneth Burke compares the story to a Platonic dialogue in which the movement is from apparent conclusions in a world of "conditions," to a world of essences, a world in which is to be found "the unconditioned," or God. "Three Definitions: The Joyce Portrait," *Kenyon Review* 8 (Spring, 1951): 191–192. For David Daiches, "The Dead" works out the theme of "a man's withdrawal into the circle of his own egotism . . . [with] those walls finally being broken down by the culminating assault on his egotism coming simultaneously from without, as an incident affecting him, and from within, as an increase of understanding." *The Novel and the Modern World* (Chicago, 1960), p. 74. That Joyce posits an "idealistic" universe is a supposition for which Burke offers no proof. Concerning Daiches's view, one must disagree with the assumption of Gabriel's egotism when it would appear that in fact he struggles *for* egotism throughout the story. True, external factors affect Gabriel,

parts in the first three stories, Gabriel anticipates the paralysis which will befall him. Like Maria, Eveline, and Mr. Duffy, he isolates himself in an imaginative celibacy. Like Lenehan and Little Chandler, like Jimmy Doyle and Farrington, Gabriel's paralysis comes on him progressively as a feeling of inferiority. With Doran and Hoppy Holohan, Gabriel gets what he wants by frustrating what he seems to want, and like Holohan and his friends, Gabriel unconsciously works to torment others, particularly his wife, Gretta. In "The Dead," the paralysis of Dublin's public life shown in "Ivy Day in the Committee Room" and in "Grace," expands to include "all the living and the dead."

"The Dead" relates Gabriel Conroy's appearance, with his wife Gretta, at his aunts' annual New Year's party. Aroused by his wife as the party ends, he looks forward to being alone with her in a Dublin hotel. However, his mood changes to diffidence and disillusion when he learns his wife had been recalling to mind a girlhood lover, Michael Furey, who had long ago died of pneumonia after standing outside her window one stormy night. Gabriel balances himself so delicately on the fine wire of his relations with other people that he expects to fall. Throughout the story, personal encounters disturb his poise until finally he gives in to the annihilation he has not only anticipated but invited. With relief, in the end, Gabriel acquiesces in the descent of universal annihilation. But out of the ashes will arise the stronger spirit of Stephen Dedalus in *A Portrait of the Artist* and *Ulysses*.

The incidents which convince Gabriel of what he has feared are his contacts with women, from the first blunder with Lily the caretaker's daughter, to his last conversation with distracted Gretta. In the course of the story he goes from one distracted woman to an-

---

but these gradually convince him of his doom. For Daiches to speak of Gabriel as "egotistical" is to take the false image he has of himself as an angelic figure for the terribly vulnerable boy-man who regards the world as he regards himself, with a "puzzled expression."

other. Gabriel's anticipation of doom is forecast when, to Lily's question "—Is it snowing again?" he replies, "—Yes, Lily . . . and I think we're in for a night of it" (p. 177). Literally he means the snow will fall all night, but he refers also to the impending social affair of his aunts, for self-conscious Gabriel not an altogether joyful prospect: he is mindful also of the universal fate of man—unending night after death of the spirit. This final meaning becomes clear in the end when Gabriel realizes that annihilation befalls everyone.

He soon hears the first hint of what he thinks of as his own fate in life, to be the victim of the corrosive sensitivities of a woman. Gabriel's lot is to offend Lily without seeming to mean it. His offense evokes Lily's cold-hearted aphorism about the animality of men which later Gabriel seems to take personally. When he asks her if she is to be married, Lily "bitterly" replies, "—The men that is now is only all palaver and what they can get out of you" (p. 178). Later Gabriel feels for Gretta a "lust" he is ashamed of when he thinks of having idealized "his own clownish lusts" (p. 220). The connection between his final shame and the early statement of Lily (the symbolically "pure" woman) is not accidental.

Having been "discomposed by [Lily's] bitter and sudden retort" (p. 179), Gabriel regains his composure by thinking of higher things: his speech, the poetry of Browning, his feeling that these would be "above the heads of his hearers" (p. 179). However, this transcendent pose is not his true disposition; he really feels that "he would fail" (p. 179).

⊙ Brought down by Lily who is beneath him socially, Gabriel finds even more unbearable his humiliation by Miss Ivors, unlike anyone else in the story his intellectual equal. Lily's retort unwittingly refers to Gabriel's lust in the end of "The Dead." But Miss Ivor's disturbs him in the one area where he might feel secure, his intellectual superiority to the others. His encounter with her is an "ordeal which was making a blush invade his forehead" (p. 189). He feels that "she had tried to make him ridiculous before people, heckling him and staring at him with her rabbit's eyes" (p. 190). He feels so much at her mercy that when she abruptly leaves the party his relief is manifest in "sudden animation" (p. 196).

Gabriel's conviction that he is at the mercy of women may be found in the symbolic complex implicit in Joyce's description of the musicale, shortly after Gabriel's arrival. In "The Sisters," the women offered a symbolic Mass to take over the role yielded by old Father Flynn. In "The Dead," the sisters (particularly Julia) and Mary Jane, celebrate a liturgical ceremony which Gabriel, the victim, uncomfortably observes. The imagery suggests a ritual of sacrifice. As she plays Mary Jane's hands are "lifted from [the piano] at the pauses like those of a priestess in momentary imprecation" (p. 186). During Mary Jane's recital, Gabriel's eyes wander to the pictures above the piano, both of which portray the tragic death which befell respectively victims of society and victims of a perverse authority: "Gabriel's eyes, irritated by the floor, which glittered with beeswax under the heavy chandelier, wandered to the wall above the piano. A picture of the balcony scene in *Romeo and Juliet* hung there and beside it was a picture of the murdered princes in the Tower which Aunt Julia had worked in red, blue and brown wools when she was a girl. Probably in the school they had gone to as girls that kind of work had been taught" (p. 186). The irritation of Gabriel's eyes suggests his discomfort at beholding the ritualization of his own plight. That Aunt Julia worked the picture of the murdered princes links her with his victimization. The idea recurs in Gabriel's after-dinner speech when he pointedly remarks that he and the other guests have gathered around "the hospital board," a symbolic altar, to be the "recipients—or perhaps, I had better say, the victims—of the hospitality of certain good ladies" (p. 202). In the context of Gabriel's feeling a victim, this remark bears a special irony. /

But Gabriel is not only a victim. Joyce also presents him in the role of the annoyingly solicitous father and husband; his family the victim of petty harassments. Recounting his imposition of a series of discomforts on the family, Gretta reveals her husband as a subtle though apparently well-meaning tormentor, a revelation of which he gruffly disapproves. "He's really an awful bother, what with green shades for Tom's eyes at night and making him do the dumb-bells, and forcing Eva to eat the stirabout. The poor child! And she simply hates the sight of it!" (p. 180). Although Gretta says all this in a bantering tone, Gabriel replies shortly afterwards to something she says "as if he were slightly angered" (p. 181).

For the rest of the party, Gabriel behaves towards Gretta with almost invariable coldness. Just after his second humiliation at the hands of Miss Ivors, Gabriel is especially icy about Gretta's enthusiasm at the prospect of a trip to Galway: "His wife clasped her hands excitedly and gave a little jump. —O, do go, Gabriel, she cried. I'd love to see Galway again. —You can go if you like, said Gabriel coldly. She looked at him for a moment, then turned to Mrs Malins and said: —There's a nice husband for you, Mrs Malins" (p. 191). His hostile attitude towards Gretta comes to a head in the room at the Hotel Gresham when gradually he replaces his short-lived ardor with a tone of "cold interrogation" (p. 220), prompted by her recollections of Michael Furey. Gabriel's icy aloofness from Gretta grows out of his angelic role which, in turn, results from an elaborate sadomasochistic pose.

As the angel Gabriel, he is a medium between the spirit world and that of the living, calling the dead from their graves as he will summon Michael Furey into the hotel room.[8] As an "angel" he must also see to the quenching of his human "lust," which requires

[8] Florence L. Walzl studies in detail the angelic imagery in "The Dead." She concludes that, though he was not completely consistent, Joyce intended Gabriel's association with the archangel who represents God's beneficence, Michael Furey with the angel who represents God's sternness. Gabriel Conroy, to whom Michael Furey brings judgment, achieves a life-giving insight at the end. Therefore, "The Dead" is "a story of maturation, tracing the spiritual development of a man from insularity and egotism to humanitarianism and love." Her essay also contains a useful summary and listing of critical interpretations of this story. Florence L. Walzl, "Gabriel and Michael: The Conclusion of 'The Dead.'" *James Joyce Quarterly* 4, no. 1 (Fall, 1966): 17–31.

the summoning of Michael Furey to archangelic tasks—both putting down rebellious Satan and barring Paradisal gates. In this role, Michael Furey quenches Gabriel's lust and bars him from the Eden of marital affection, because Gabriel had summoned him from death to fulfill his angelic mission. The angelic superstructure veils and expresses the more homely possibility that Gabriel sabotages his relationship with Gretta because he listens to the voice of his dead mother. Her "sullen opposition" to his marriage becomes his own. He must live according to the wishes of the living dead; the mask of god he wears is that of his dead mother, hypnotizing him into acting out her taboo against his marriage.[9] His compulsive engineering of Gretta into "betraying" him with another man has masochistic archetypes, but it might well stem from the spell of the dead, mesmerizing him, as Dublin is mesmerized. When he "ascends" the stairs in the Hotel Gresham, "He could have flung his arms about her hips and held her still for his arms were trembling with desire to seize her" (p. 215). He feels a desperate urge for affection before the internal taboo can operate. The old porter accompanies them with the candle, an image for Gabriel's sexual desire: "The porter halted on the stairs to settle his guttering candle. They halted too on the steps below him. In the silence Gabriel could hear the falling of the molten wax into the tray and the thumping of his own heart against his ribs" (p. 215).[10] But the

[9] Gabriel's flight from involvement with Gretta is suggested by the analogy with Bret Harte's novel *Gabriel Conroy*. In this novel, Ashley and Grace escape from their snowbound party in the high Sierras and, although they seem romantically involved, when their escape from death is assured, Ashley deviously flees the girl as soon as possible, completely abandoning her. Gerhard Friedrich has pointed out that Joyce probably got the name for his character from the Harte novel, and has noted also the similarity between the famous last paragraph of "The Dead" and the first paragraph of *Gabriel Conroy*, both of which contain striking descriptions of snow. I agree with Friederich about these two similarities; I would add, however, that there is a further resemblance between the stories in that Gabriel also "flees" Gretta, though not in a way as obvious as that in which Ashley abandons Grace. "Bret Harte as a Source for James Joyce's 'The Dead,' " *Philological Quarterly* 33 (October, 1954): 442–444.

[10] Elsewhere in *Dubliners* candles and candle flames have erotic significance,

candle is already "guttering," melting as rapidly as Gabriel's lust.
And when they arrive at the door of their room, the porter sets "his
unstable candle down," as though Gabriel's sex were unstable also.
Gabriel's next act is to refuse light: "—We don't want any light. We
have light enough from the street." He must dismiss the candle
which represents his carnal feeling: "You might remove that handsome article, like a good man" (p. 216).[11] Understandably, the porter
"was surprized by such a novel idea" (p. 216). In lieu of the flame
of his own affection, Gabriel prefers the light from the street: "A
ghostly light from the street lamp lay in a long shaft from one window to the door . . . He looked down into the street in order that
his emotion might calm a little" (p. 216). The "ghostly" light represents Michael Furey, the expectant ghost, who once worked for
the gas company, invited into the room at Gabriel's behest to succor
the wife whose disaffection Gabriel has already subtly evoked. "She
turned away from the mirror slowly and walked along the shaft of
light towards him. Her face looked so serious and weary that the
words would not pass Gabriel's lips. No, it was not the moment yet"
(p. 216). Gabriel waits, "fearing that diffidence was about to con-
quer him," and "in a false voice," he initiates a discussion about
Freddy Malins, more obviously than Gabriel a toady to his mother.
Gretta's "abstracted" response soon causes Gabriel to tremble with
annoyance (p. 217). He can now feel justified in his refusal to trans-
gress the internal taboo because an indignant anger has moved into
him evoked by the abstraction from him which he had engendered
in Gretta. His tender ardor changes shortly to a brutal vehemence:

as in "A Little Cloud," in which the name of the central character, Little
Chandler, has a derisive sexual significance. In "The Boarding House," an
erotic play with lighted candles precedes the consummation of the relationship of Polly and Doran: candle flames in that story refer obviously to sexual
arousal (p. 67).

[11] Brewster Ghiselin notes Gabriel's dismissal of the candle as "perhaps his
wish to be lighted only by the fire of his joy." "The Unity of Joyce's *Dubliners*,"
Accent 16 (1956): 210. This interpretation, which confuses the literal and the
symbolic, fails to render the story more intelligible. For one thing, Gabriel's
"joy" diminishes when the door is closed.

"He longed to cry to her from his soul, to crush her body against his, to overmaster her" (p. 217). Her unexpected kiss pacifies him briefly: "trembling with delight" he wonders "why he had been so diffident" (pp. 217–218). He draws her gently towards him and softly says, "—Gretta, dear, what are you thinking about?" (p. 218). His question is just about the final move in a game to achieve both his frustration and hers, and of course this question leads to the revelation about Michael Furey. A consummate pretender, Gabriel has in the course of a few minutes played every role, from tender lover to indignant husband; from imperious conquest to humble understanding. As one of the living dead, his final role is in his identification with the dead: "His soul swooned slowly as he heard the snow falling faintly through the universe and faintly falling, like the descent of their last end, upon all the living and the dead" (p. 224). But his "true" self, behind the poses and the hypnotic compulsive sadomasochism is a wistful and sympathetic desire for affection.

He does love Gretta, in a neurotic way. Forbidden in this by a repressed injunction, possibly his own mother's opposition, he must both express and feel affection in devious ways, by identification: by "feeling into" the experience of others, in this case Michael Furey who had loved Gretta as Gabriel would if he could. For this reason, even more than out of jealousy, Gabriel feels a wistful envy for Michael Furey who could do what Gabriel feels forbidden to do. Like a small boy he envies those who have been allowed contact with the living fire of life.

Gabriel's final attitude towards Gretta is a compound of affection and hostility. His summoning of Michael Furey is an expression and denial of affection for his wife. He wishes to live with her as a lover by feeling into Michael's experience and hers as well, so he summons Michael as a lover. But he also summons Michael both as avenging angel and successful rival and in these roles Michael successfully bars the gates of Eden. Thus the hostility Gabriel feels for Gretta finds an effective mythical and psychological structure.

But even his "hostility" is a pretense. He may be acting out his mother's sullen opposition when he opposes Gretta's wish to travel in Galway. But, if so, he does not feel this hostility so much as he feels himself into his mother's feeling of it through contact with her in death. Just as his love must be experienced through Michael Furey, his contempt must be experienced through his mother. Thus he must pretend to despise Galway, which he associates with Gretta and with his mother's contempt for her "country cuteness."

Miss Ivors, with "her critical quizzing eyes" disturbs him because she senses the pretense of his anti-Irish feeling, which she cannot imagine to be natural. Gabriel acts out this contempt as compulsively as he acts out his hostility for Gretta. This feeling too may grow out of his dancing to the tune of maternal opposition. Thus he would validly perceive himself the victim of feminine torture. While he listens to Mary Jane's tormenting if not "thought-tormented" music, his eyes wander to the wall and he sees the embroidered rituals of sacrifice. Playing the piano like a "priestess," Mary Jane figures among the series of women for whom Gabriel has been a priestly sacrifice, as he says, a victim "of the hospitality of certain good women." Above the piano, Gabriel beholds scenes reminiscent of his own victimization. The murdered princes and Romeo and Juliet were barred from the exercise of their rights. Because of the psychopathic hatred and ambition of their hunch-backed uncle, the princes were deprived of their kingdom. Romeo and Juliet were victims of the active opposition of feuding parents. Gabriel, who has the makings of a king, is reduced to being the tool of his aunts. He should be the affectionate conqueror of his wife but his acquiescence in the tyranny of repression shatters his conjugal imperium. Immediately after looking at the pictures "a shadow passed over his face as he remembered [his mother's] sullen opposition to his marriage" (p. 187). Typically, he denies in his reflections her description of Gretta as "country cute." It is enough for him to deny to himself what he must act out in his relation with his wife.

Shortly after leaving the party, Gabriel has imagined Gretta as the subject for a painting he would call "Distant Music." As she stands listening to "The Lass of Aughrim," which triggers her recollection of Michael Furey, Gabriel considers converting her into a symbol: "What is a woman standing on the stairs in the shadow, listening to distant music, a symbol of" (p. 210). His subsequent memories of their early life together are recollections of his own feelings—she has provided material for his highly aesthetic sensibility: "Moments of their secret life together burst like stars upon his memory. A heliotrope envelope was lying beside his breakfast-cup and he was caressing it with his hand" (p. 213). He recalls writing in a letter to her: "*Why is it that words like these seem to me so dull and cold? Is it because there is no word tender enough to be your name?*" (p. 214). One aspect of Gabriel's need to defend himself against the deep human involvement with Gretta, suggested by his preference for the snow and the cold, is his pose as an aesthete. Like Stephen with Emma at the end of *A Portrait*, Gabriel turns on "the spiritual-heroic refrigerating apparatus, invented and patented in all countries by Dante" (*Portrait*, p. 252). Poetry preserves the self by freezing human response, which in Dublin can lead to damnation. But, employed defensively in human affairs, art also destroys. In this connection, the well-known influence on Joyce of the later Ibsen may be clearly sensed.[12] In *When We Dead Awaken*, the sculptor Rubek has employed art to defend himself against sexual involvement with his model, Irene. By means of an aesthetic vampirism, he "steals" her soul and embodies it in the sculpture which Irene comes to regard as their "child." Subsequently, she turns to other men, and finally becomes one of the living dead. Years later, when they meet, she accuses him: "I hated you ... When I stripped myself naked and stood there before you ... because you could stand there so utterly passionless

[12] See especially, James R. Baker, "Ibsen, Joyce, and the Living Dead" in *A James Joyce Miscellany*, third series, ed. Marvin Magalaner (Carbondale, 1962), pp. 19–32.

and unmoved . . . and because you were an artist—only an artist—
and not a man."[13] She feels that in sacrificing herself for his art,
she had committed suicide. Too late, he repents his own mistake.
Thus, Ibsen rejects a total dedication to art which would eliminate
human response. However, Rubek and Irene die in an avalanche
which has been compared with the falling of the snow at the end
of "The Dead." In *When We Dead Awaken*, the avalanche signi-
fies the ultimate destructiveness not only of single-minded aestheti-
cism, but of a tardy involvement in human relationships. Their
"resurrection" is only possible through a transfiguration achieved
by the artistic imagination. In climbing together the snow-covered
mountain, Rubek and Irene display themselves before the forces
of good and evil. They rise above them: "All the forces of light are
welcome to look upon us. And the powers of darkness, too."[14] They
are symbols for late nineteenth-century aesthetic hysteria: their
transfiguration the final illusion.

It would be as inaccurate to picture Gabriel Conroy as an egotistical, Rubek-like voyeur as it would be to picture him as a self-
centered bourgeois sensualist. Of course, he is both of these, but
neither essentially. His voyeurism, his sensuality, even his own
self-accusation, his idealization of "his own clownish lusts" (p. 220)
—these are poses by which he can deny the genuineness of his affection, denials of his deeper sense of humanity. Self-flagellation de-
fends him from what he really seeks—to love his wife—perhaps
because the repressed maternal injunction informing his false conscience must be appeased. He resembles Mr. James Duffy in "A
Painful Case," who typifies the corrosive conscience of Ireland: a
system of pernicious injunctions from parents and clergy, the tyrannical "gods" of Dublin who inhibit human response. In *A Portrait
of the Artist as a Young Man*, Stephen will try to understand and
reject these injunctions in himself and thus be in the way of creating

---

[13] Henrik Ibsen, *When We Dead Awaken*, in *Last Plays of Henrik Ibsen*,
trans. Arvid Paulson (New York, 1962), p. 412.

[14] *Ibid.*, p. 431.

a new conscience for his race. His effort will be ambiguously successful. In *Ulysses*, Stephen's desperate struggle with his mother's ghost, who implores him to accede to her wishes, culminates in the smashing of a brothel light, his "sin" against the false and mercenary "light" of Dublin. His cry, "Non Serviam," is a rejection of the "gods" of Dublin, requiring that he assume the role of Satan.

Gabriel Conroy cannot yet utter so astounding a denial of the complicated role his artificial conscience requires of him. Pretentious lover and reluctant husband, he cannot yet affirm without fear what he really feels. But he is very close to being a Joycean hero. First he must suffer annihilating agonies in the Hotel Gresham. These agonies are a prelude to the destruction of Dublin's neurotic conscience.

CHAPTER V

Exiles: A Rough and Tumble Between de Sade and Sacher-Masoch

"When you are a recognized classic people will read it because you wrote it and be duly interested and duly instructed, . . . but until then I'm hang'd if I see what's to be done with it." Ezra Pound to James Joyce, 6–12 September 1915, *Pound/Joyce.*

"*Exiles* is the final epiphany of the material organized epically in *Dubliners.*" Hugh Kenner, "Joyce's *Exiles.*"

Critics see Joyce's play *Exiles* as his single failure, an opinion borne out by the infrequency of its performance. Aside from the apparent inability of *Exiles* to fulfill the conditions of its genre, the play remains an enigma which, writes Robert Adams, "has . . . regularly baffled and frustrated admirers to whom the intricacies of *Finnegans Wake* seem . . . child's play."[1] Written between *A Portrait of the Artist as a Young Man* and *Ulysses*, *Exiles* must have been a significant phase in Joyce's development. As Harry Levin has noted: "Richard [Rowan's] dilemma is a restatement of Stephen's; and, though the play is less autobiographical than the novel, it sketches a self-portrait at a later period."[2]

Whether one perceives *Exiles* as an autobiographical statement or as a unique if puzzling dramatic situation, one should examine Joyce's depiction of complex human behavior in conjunction with

[1] Robert Adams, "Light on Joyce's *Exiles*? A New MS, a Curious Analogue, and Some Speculations." *Studies in Bibliography* 17 (1964): 83.

[2] Harry Levin in *The Portable James Joyce* (New York, 1959), p. 528.

the question of the artistic character of the play. In the end, one might either comprehend more accurately why the play fails, or one might come to think the play no failure after all. My view is that in *Exiles* Joyce inventively portrayed a pervasive theme as I have described it in *Dubliners*: the self lives slavishly through the experience of others, freely through direct involvement with the real. Joyce both explored and opposed exclusively vicarious experience; exploited and rejoiced in it. Earlier I have described an obsession with this form of experience as a feature of sadomasochistic neurosis. The concepts used in my explication of *Dubliners* have even more relevance to *Exiles*, which Joyce himself described as "a rough and tumble between the Marquis de Sade and Freiherr v. Sacher Masoch."[3]

Just back in Ireland from nine years in Italy, Richard Rowan meets again Beatrice Justice with whom he had corresponded for eight of the years and, a little later, her cousin Robert Hand, a journalist with whom Richard had once caroused. Robert has come to arrange an evening meeting between Richard and the university vice-chancellor, who will offer him a chair of romance languages. He has come also to schedule an evening assignation with Richard's common-law wife Bertha.[4] In accordance with a mutual policy of complete openness, after Robert leaves, Bertha reveals the plan to

[3] Joyce, "Notes by the Author," *Exiles* (New York, 1965), p. 124. Subsequent references to the notes and to the play will be from this edition and will be noted in parentheses after the quotations.

[4] Joyce left it unclear whether Bertha and Richard are married at the time of the action in *Exiles*. Clearly, they had gone off to the continent unmarried. Richard speaks of old Mrs. Rowan's objections concerning his "nameless" child, which implies that Archie is illegitimate (*Exiles*, p. 24). However, Joyce also wrote in the notes of Richard's wish to experience adultery vicariously through the affair between Robert and Bertha (Notes, p. 125). Since Robert is unmarried, this would imply that Bertha must be married. But the *dramatis personae* lists only "Bertha," not that she is Richard Rowan's wife. From all of this it appears to me that Bertha and Richard are not legally or sacramentally married, but they look upon themselves as husband and wife nevertheless. I suppose it is accurate enough, then, to refer to Bertha as Richard's common-law wife."

Richard, who suavely encourages her to fulfill it. That evening, as Robert prepares to receive Bertha, Richard appears, casually reveals his knowledge of their pending liaison and, again, subtly urges Robert to consummate it. Richard departs, Bertha enters, admits to the stunned Robert her revelation to Richard. After a long, increasingly passionate discussion, they embrace. But, as the scene ends, it is unclear whether Bertha will spend the night or leave at once.[5]

The next morning, Bertha, at home, distraught, receives Beatrice who brings a newspaper essay by Robert heralding the return from exile of Richard, and the news that Robert has prepared to leave immediately for England. As they talk, Bertha reveals an affection for Beatrice. Beatrice leaves, Robert enters, declares to Bertha he "dreamed" the consummation of their affair the previous night. Bertha exits, Richard enters. Robert recounts the previous night to him. After Bertha left, he visited pubs, picked up a woman, had intercourse with her ("a death of the spirit") in a cab. He returned home, wrote the essay, packed for his journey. The play ends with a dialogue between Bertha and Richard. She declares her unbroken fidelity; he announces his "wounding doubt." Apparently, they will achieve the reconciliation she desires, holding Richard's hand as he lies down exhausted on a lounge. Like Gabriel in the conclusion

---

[5] Critics have usually avoided this question, which I take to be crucial. In his recent extended commentary on *Exiles*, Darcy O'Brien does not even discuss it. *The Conscience of James Joyce* (Princeton, 1968), pp. 55–69. Before him, neither Pound nor Kenner questioned whether Robert and Bertha actually sleep together. Robert Adams says that they "keep an assignation" but does not actually say they have intercourse. Adams, "Light on Joyce's *Exiles*," p. 84. In his notes, Joyce seems to have wished the audience to be in doubt. "The doubt which clouds the end of the play must be conveyed to the audience not only through Richard's questions to both but also from the dialogue between Robert and Bertha" (Notes, p. 125). However, he also wrote: "All believe that Bertha is Robert's mistress. This *belief* rubs against his own *knowledge* of what has been, but he accepts the belief as a bitter food" (Notes, p. 123). I take this to mean that at the end of Act II, Bertha leaves immediately. Robert is left frustrated, hence his bitterness. When he tells Bertha he "dreamed" their consummation he means just that. In Act III, his recounting to Robert the events of the evening should be taken at face value. In *Exiles* practically all of the sexual "action" takes place in the characters' imaginations.

of "The Dead," who also reclines wearily after having engineered his own betrayal, and like Bloom at the end of *Ulysses*, who lies down beside faithless Molly, by the end of *Exiles*, Richard Rowan has earned a Joycean rest, fulfilled by Earwicker's nearly perpetual somnolence throughout *Finnegans Wake*. Like Bloom, Richard is weary. He has traveled through several modes of experience.

Ostensibly, *Exiles* dramatizes Richard Rowan's confrontation with conventional morality, which permits adultery only within a context of subterfuge. All parties to an adulterous liaison must either deceive their partners or friends, or they must play a game of deception however much their activities are known. Richard's insistence on openness confronts bourgeois morality, not by approving of adultery, but by disapproving of subterfuge; not by insisting on indiscriminate sexual liaisons, but by advocating freedom of sexual choice. Described in this way, *Exiles* might seem a dramatization of Nietzschean overstatement. It might have proved a serious artistic contribution to modern marital ethics, in the spirit of *A Doll's House*. But a play which could have tried the brain of Ezra Pound cannot be said simply to have dealt in a clear-cut way with an important if unorthodox issue.[6] Hypocrisy and its attendant evils were within the target of Joyce's articulate contempt, as they have been for most artists. But if one sees the play chiefly as the dramatization of a conflict between middle-class morality and Joyce's advocacy of freedom and openness, one must view *Exiles* as a failure. In fact, the assault on bourgeois hypocrisy and marital commercialism serves *in the play* to rationalize the obsessive humour of Richard Rowan. Joyce could never have remained content even with the exposition of libertarian pieties.

Richard Rowan's attack against the bourgeois concept of sexual morality fits into the system of partial truths and libertarian

---

[6] "Roughly speaking, it takes about all the brains I've got to take the thing, *reading*. And I suppose I've . . . more intelligence than the normal theatre goer (god save us)." *Pound/Joyce: The Letters of Ezra Pound to James Joyce, with Pound's Essays on Joyce*, ed. with commentary by Forrest Read (New York, 1967), p. 45.

clichés he uses to deceive himself, Bertha, and his friends about the sadomasochistic project which, as with most of Joyce's Dubliners, constitutes Richard's aim in *Exiles*. The evidence for this view abounds in the play and in Joyce's notes on *Exiles*. Richard acts to achieve vicariously his own abasement and that of Bertha and Robert, just as he needs to feel alive through their real or imagined sexual vitality. In this aim he is controlled by spiritual allegiance to his dead mother, his instructor in the techniques of sadomasochism. Thus, his project resembles that of Gabriel in "The Dead."

In his notes, Joyce succinctly defined Richard's quest: "Richard unfitted for adulterous intercourse with the wives of his friends because it would involve a great deal of pretence on his part rather than because he is convinced of any dishonorableness in it wishes, it seems, to feel the thrill of adultery vicariously and to possess a bound woman Bertha through the organ of his friend" (p. 125). The statement suggests both the element of neurotic rationalization and neurotic wish-fulfillment in the play. Richard is "unfitted for adulterous intercourse" not out of any defect in himself, or out of moral disapprobation, but because however amoral he is a devotee of openness. Though his pronouncements would bear this flattering opinion out, his actual behavior does little to establish a devotion to openness, much to establish his reliance on imposture and subterfuge. As Hugh Kenner noted, "*Exiles* explores a counterposition of modes of insincerity."[7] The neurotic element in Richard, Joyce describes in the rest of his statement. Intercourse with Bertha could hardly be adulterous. But vicarious intercourse with her by imagining the experience of his friend would be adulterous because it would mean becoming his adulterous friend. One could hardly imagine a pretence more intricate than wishing to be an adulterous friend with one's own sexual partner. Thus, the reason which Joyce advances for Richard's unfitness for adultery, his aversion for pretence, may be in part a rationalization, though to cover precisely which desire is difficult to decide. Therefore, it is important to as-

[7] Hugh Kenner, "Joyce's *Exiles*," *Hudson Review* 5 (Autumn, 1952): 390.

certain in *Exiles* the specific quest of Richard that informs it as a
drama, referring throughout to Joyce's notes, though they are only
slightly less cryptic than the play itself. Beginning with such an analysis, one can reassess *Exiles* as a work of dramatic art, and perhaps
help explain and relieve the understandable bewilderment of critics
from Ezra Pound onwards. As Robert Adams has noted:

> The reader's problems with *Exiles* are primarily problems of moti-
> vation, not of episode . . . We do not know for sure that Richard
> wants the chair of romance literature; we do not know whether
> Robert wants him to have it, or why. We may be certain that if
> Richard loves Beatrice Justice (as Bertha vigorously insists he does),
> it is in a pretty remote and theoretical way; but how does this love,
> or any other consideration involving Miss Justice, contribute to this
> conclusion? What is, in fact, the nature of this conclusion? It is
> clear that the departure of Robert represents the end of a threat;
> but the end of the play is by no means the triumph of true love.
> Richard says it is not. It is not in the darkness of belief that he now
> desires Bertha; he desires her "in restless living wounding doubt,"
> and proposes . . . to reestablish his menage on that basis. There is a
> preliminary problem here as to what he is talking about; there is a
> further question whether, when we understand him, we can prevent
> him from seeming a Narcissistic prig. On all these scores, *Exiles*
> represents an outstanding piece of unfinished Joycean business.[8]

One may begin to decipher Richard's motivation by thinking
of it as the desire to resolve a conflict which is "in" himself. This
acting for resolution of a conflict; this *"agon"* defines Richard as a
protagonist. One may express it by following a hint from Francis
Fergusson's *Idea of a Theatre*: that is, to express the "action" in a
play by an infinitive phrase.[9] Thus, the "action" in *Oedipus Rex*,
for example, might be expressed in the phrase "to find the culprit."[10]
Several infinitive phrases might render the action in *Exiles*. In the
preceding plot summary of *Exiles*, the infinitive most appropriate

---

[8] Adams, "Light on Joyce's *Exiles*," pp. 84–85.
[9] Francis Fergusson, *The Idea of a Theatre* (New York, 1953), p. 244.
[10] *Ibid.*

might read: "to stage his own betrayal." Insofar as Richard acts for this immediate end, he may also be said to act for a purpose more remote: "To rise above bourgeois morality," in spirt of what Hugh Kenner describes as that of exiles "above the spiritual snowline," who "adhere to the Ibsen-Wagner-Nietzsche image of liberated life."[11] But I have suggested that this infinitive serves as a rationalization of Richard's true aims. Here psychoanalytic perception helps focus what Joyce put into the play, that Richard's aim is to act out the wishes of his dead mother. Therefore, it is a matter of determining not only what Richard wants, but what his mother wants him to want. Like Richard, we must proceed to an interrogation of spirits.

In *Exiles,* the decision to act according to his mother's wishes does not occur until Richard has resolved in himself a "conflict" between the spirit of his father and mother dramatized through dialogue early in the first act. Richard has been talking with Beatrice Justice, whom he has not seen for nine years, though they had corresponded for the past eight. He has questioned her about their relationship. He has exerted on her a hypnotic effect she cannot define. In his life, in his recently published book, and in his letters to her, he has expressed something in her soul which she could not express for lack of courage. He has been preoccupied with her soul because of Beatrice's childhood pledge of love to Robert Hand. In this way, early in *Exiles* Joyce establishes Richard's inclination to project himself imaginatively into a *menage a trois,* in this case going back many years. Though later his obsession will work within the Richard-Bertha-Robert triangle, here early in the play he reveals an involvement in a triangle involving Beatrice instead of Bertha. His final diagnosis of Beatrice's plight is that, "You were drawn to him as your mind was drawn towards mine. You held back from him. From me, too, in a different way. You cannot give yourself freely and wholly" (p. 22). This diagnosis leads to Richard's first self-revelation: "O, if you knew how I am suffering at this moment! For your case, too. But suffering most of all for my own. *With bitter*

[11] Kenner, "Joyce's *Exiles,*" p. 397.

force. And how I pray that I may be granted again my dead mother's hardness of heart! For some help, within me or without, I must find. And find it I will" (p. 22).

From the ensuing dialogue with Beatrice, it is clear that Richard's mother had bitterly opposed both his relationship with Bertha and his defection from the Church. Though on her deathbed she had urged him to break with his past, he had remained unmoved, like Stephen Dedalus. The meaning of his prayer to be granted *again* his dead mother's hardness of heart, is that he had used against her on her deathbed the same hardness she had used against him. Typically Joycean, she indoctrinated Richard in the policy of meanness. He wishes to be granted again the hardness of her spirit, not now solely against her but in league with her against his present "enemies," the "disciples"—Bertha and Robert—with faith great enough to betray him (p. 44). Like James Duffy, in "A Painful Case," Eveline in "Eveline," Gabriel in "The Dead"; like Stephen in *Ulysses*, Richard will act out parental hard-heartedness from a feeling of guilty pity, queasy remorse, and sadistic meanness. This tortured motivation he expresses to Beatrice: "*fiercely*: How can my words hurt her poor body that rots in the grave? Do you think I do not pity her cold blighted love for me? I fought against her spirit while she lived to the bitter end. *He presses his hand to his forehead*. It fights against me still—in here" (p. 23). However he does not undertake an unseating of her internal tyranny so much as he enlists her spirit in a tyranny of his own, by which he acquiesces in a maternal imperium he had once opposed. He will be, in Hugh Kenner's terms, "a lonely deity," who "must on principle dominate everyone."[12] His mood compares with that of Stephen in "Nestor," looking down on his young pupil in Deasy's school. After a meditation on mother's love, "the only true thing in life," Stephen thinks: "My childhood bends beside me, too far for me to lay a hand there once or lightly. Mine is far and his secret as our eyes. Secrets, silent, stony sit in the dark palaces of both our hearts:

12 *Ibid.*, p. 395.

secrets weary of their tyranny: tyrants willing to be dethroned" (*Ulysses*, p. 28). Richard's declaration to Beatrice leads to a brief struggle between his sympathetic inclinations, identified with the spirit of his "smiling handsome father" (whose picture is on the wall), and the hardness he derives from the cold spirit of his mother. This is a final phase in his determination towards severity. The recollection of his mother's rage against him precipitates a brief conflict in which there are elements of contempt and admiration: "There were tongues here ready to tell her all, to embitter her withering mind still more against me and Bertha and our godless nameless child. *Holding out his hands to her.* Can you not hear her mocking me while I speak? You must know the voice, surely, the voice that called you 'the black protestant,' the pervert's daughter. *With sudden selfcontrol.* In any case a remarkable woman" (p. 24).

In his voice, Richard expects Beatrice to hear the voice of his mother, which establishes the extent to which she is "in" him and to which he must commit himself to acting out the wishes of her spirit. But he must pay homage also to the gentler spirit of his father: "*approaching, touches her lightly on the shoulder, and points to the crayon drawing on the wall*: Do you see him there, smiling and handsome? His last thoughts! I remember the night he died. *He pauses for an instant and then goes on calmly.* I was a boy of fourteen. He called me to his bedside. He knew I wanted to go to the theatre to hear *Carmen*. He told my mother to give me a shilling. I kissed him and went. When I came home he was dead. Those were his last thoughts as far as I know" (p. 24).

In Richard's imagination, two deathbed scenes are constantly alive. The dead parents struggle unceasingly for resurrection in the voice of their living son, by which struggle they are truely the "living dead." Richard soon resolves the conflict between the gentle spirit of his father and the fierce ghost of his mother: "*gazing again at the drawing, calmly, almost gaily*: He will help me, perhaps, my smiling handsome father" (p. 25). At this point Robert's knock is heard. Richard says, "No. No. Not the smiler, Miss Justice. The old mother. It is her spirit I need. I am going" (p. 25). This spirit he hears throughout *Exiles*. She tells him what to do and she steels his soul in the undertaking. Richard's identification more with the maternal than with the paternal principle is apparent in a manuscript fragment Joyce originally wrote to be included in Act II in a scene between Richard and Robert. Here he explicitly perceives himself in an embryologically maternal role and he puts aside Robert's application of the paternal to him:

> ROBERT: . . . You are so young and yet you seem to be her [Bertha's] father and mine.
> RICHARD: . . . you say I am like her father. Do you know what I feel when I look at her?
> ROBERT: What?
> RICHARD: I feel as if I had carried her within my own body, in my womb.
> ROBERT: Can a man feel like that?
> RICHARD: Her books, her music, the fire of thought stolen from on high out of whose flames all ease and culture have come, the grace with which she tends the body we desire—whose work is that? I feel that it is mine. It is my work and the work of others like me now or in other times. It is we who have conceived her and brought her forth. Our minds flowing together are the womb in which we have borne her.[13]

In this fragment, as Robert Adams observes, Richard employs "a familiar and beloved metaphor" of Joyce's, the image of the culture hero among culture heroes who creates in the womb of his own superior imagination the very creatures he desires, as was true of Stephen Dedalus in *A Portrait of the Artist*. In less exalted terms, he acts also out of identification with the "old mother" of his imagination, responsive to the ghostly ventriloquism of Mrs. Rowan.

If Richard's obsessive humour grows out of an allegiance to his dead mother, it remains to describe the operation of his humour. Then we should be able to speculate as to why his mother should

---

[13] Adams, "Light on Joyce's *Exiles*," p. 86.

wish him to act as a sadomasochist, living vicariously on the experience of his friends.

From the moment of his decision to employ the spirit of his mother, Richard behaves with a studied hardness, as Robert Hand perceives in their first dialogue: "You have your iron mask on today" (p. 38). Richard's face now wears his mother's sternness. Proceeding from a spiritual world, this severity suggests also an application to the physical world of angelic standards.[14] Once again, it is Robert Hand who divines in Richard the spiritual element which he incongruously identifies as the *saeva indignatio* of Jonathan Swift:

> ROBERT, *with animation*: You have that fierce indignation which lacerated the heart of Swift. You have fallen from a higher world, Richard, and you are filled with fierce indignation, when you find that life is cowardly and ignoble. While I . . . shall I tell you?
> RICHARD: By all means.
> ROBERT, *archly*: I have come up from a lower world and I am filled with astonishment when I find that people have any redeeming virtue at all. (pp. 43–44)

Richard does not repudiate his place in Robert's naive diagram of higher and lower worlds, nor does he openly agree with it. But his subsequent manipulation of Robert and the others indicates that he does make use of it. In this diagram, he is a fallen angel; Robert a devil. Richard is amusingly described as a Swiftean angel. But later in Act One, Bertha accuses Richard himself of "the work of a devil" (p. 51) when she discovers the plan to reveal to Robert his knowledge of their assignation. Richard does not remain celestial, nor Robert diabolical throughout. Then again, despite their pre-

[14] Kenner stresses this aspect of *Exiles*: "Ethical freedom which shall not be anarchy and utter honesty which shall not be corrosive are proper, it is not merely wry to remark, to a society of angels. Angels strictly speaking: unfallen beings of perfect rationality, in whose society there is no marrying nor giving in marriage. The Exiles to whom this perfection is impossible are exiled from Eden: that is the ultimate meaning of the play." Kenner, "Joyce's *Exiles*," p. 392.

vailing inclinations, neither is Richard consistently masochistic nor
Robert consistently sadistic, though indeed Joyce directly stated
such an interpretation in his notes. "Had not Robert better give
Bertha a little bite when they kiss? Richard's Masochism needs no
example" (p. 124).

Joyce's concept of sadism and masochism appears to have resembled the incomplete notion that they were phenomena differing
chiefly in that the sadist loves to inflict pain, the masochist to suffer it. On this level of understanding, Joyce attempts consistency.
For example, Robert enjoys pinching little Archie's ear; Richard
enjoys his own betrayal. But *Exiles* is a deeper study of sadism and
masochism than Joyce realized. His depiction of psychopathology
verifies Wilhelm Stekel's observation that sadomasochism is a single
phenomenon in which the neurotic both directs and plays con-
flicting roles:

> The great secret which other authors have already suspected, that
> we have to do with a bipolar phenomenon, becomes through the
> experiences of analysis a self-evident fact. The paraphiliac identi-
> fies himself with his object; he feels himself into it so that he can
> experience both conditions: triumph and defeat, power and sub-
> jection, activity and passivity, male and female, resistance and the
> overcoming of it. The specific scene which he is always wanting to
> repeat is a drama, a fiction, in which he as the author feels with the
> actors, suffers and enjoys.[15]

Stekel stresses the sadomasochist's compulsion towards repetition,
usually of a childhood scene he witnessed or imagined, ordinarily
involving his parents in an act of violence, perversion, or betrayal.
Thus he writes: "Sadomasochism is a form of psychosexual infantilism. The impulse shows an obsessive character and manifests
itself as a repetition compulsion. In all cases of sadomasochism we
shall find the entire instrumentarium of infantilism and with it a

[15] Wilhelm Stekel, *Sadism and Masochism: The Psychology of Hatred and
Cruelty*, vol. 1 (New York, 1963), p. 6.

well developed fetishism accompanied by its most important phenomenon, flight from the partner."[16]

Whatever psychoanalytic construction one might imagine, nothing in *Exiles* could possibly establish that Joyce portrays Richard Rowan in the process of staging the compulsive repetition of a *childhood* scene. More probably, he is under a compulsion to stage the enactment of a relatively recent scene, sharply etched in his imagination. This scene, this drama, he sets up and manipulates according to the directions of his dead mother, and to some extent the drama repeats his own experience with her as well as the command he had ignored nine years earlier. Therefore, his compulsion is to enact both what he had experienced at the time of his exile with Bertha, and what he had refused to acquiesce in on command of his mother. He must take Bertha off again through imagined participation in the experience of Robert with her, and he must reject Bertha at the behest of his mother. Like Gabriel in "The Dead," Richard stages a second honeymoon through the experience of another man with his sexual partner, according to the instructions of the dead. He becomes playwright, director, and vicarious actor in a play within a play. Old Mrs. Rowan is his muse.

For its connections with theatre, the most intriguing aspect of Richard is the quest for vicarious experience Joyce emphasizes in his notes. Richard "wishes, it seems, to feel the thrill of adultery vicariously and to possess a bound woman Bertha through the organ of his friend" (p. 125). This quest for experience at second hand is particularly apparent in Richard's interrogation of Bertha concerning the exact details of her meetings with Robert:

> BERTHA: . . . Then he caressed my hand and asked would I let him kiss it. I let him.
> RICHARD: Well?
> BERTHA: Then he asked could he embrace me—even once? . . . and Then . . .

[16] *Ibid.*, p. 59.

RICHARD: And then?
BERTHA: He put his arm around me.
RICHARD, *stares at the floor for a moment, then looks at her again*:
    And then? (p. 48)

Aware that Richard's obsession with these details is peculiar, Bertha
asks him, "Does all this disturb you?" Richard replies, "I want to
find out what he means or feels just as you do." In the spirit of
neurotic experimentation, Richard proceeds with the interrogation:

BERTHA: He asked for a kiss. I said: "Take it."
RICHARD: And then?
BERTHA, *crumpling a handful of petals*: He kissed me.
RICHARD: Your mouth?
BERTHA: Once or twice.
RICHARD: Long kisses?
BERTHA: Fairly long. *Reflects.* Yes, the last time.
RICHARD, *rubs his hands slowly; then*: With his lips? Or . . . the other
    way?
BERTHA: Yes, the last time.
RICHARD: Did he ask you to kiss him?
BERTHA: He did.
RICHARD: Did you?
BERTHA, *hesitates, then looking straight at him*: I did. I kissed him.
RICHARD: What way?
BERTHA, *with a shrug*: O simply.
RICHARD: Were you excited?
BERTHA: Well, you can imagine. *Frowning suddenly.* Not much.
    He has not nice lips . . . Still I was excited, of course. But not like
    with you, Dick.
RICHARD: Was he?
BERTHA: Excited? Yes, I think he was. He sighed. He was dreadfully
    nervous.
RICHARD, *resting his forehead on his hand*: I see. (p. 49)

The atmosphere has been that of the confessional, Richard delighting in details of the erotic behavior of a young woman, an
opportunity sought but denied to Stephen Dedalus in *Stephen
Hero* and in *A Portrait*. Much like Lenehan in "Two Gallants,"

Richard participates in a liaison between his friend and a woman by dwelling on the imagination of erotic detail. But his gratification exceeds that of Lenehan because he can interrogate the woman directly. Therefore, when Bertha admits at least one "fairly long" kiss with Robert, Richard "rubs his hands slowly," a gesture of satisfaction not granted to Lenehan or Gabriel Conroy, his predecessors in vicarious experience. His interrogative tone throughout is calm where that of Lenehan had been anxious and of Gabriel uneasy.

Despite the compulsive need for erotic detail, Richard does not require the certainty that Bertha and Robert consummate their affair. *Exiles* ends with still another inquiry, the function of which is not so much to elicit conviction as to establish doubt. Here, Bertha questions Richard:

> BERTHA: It is not true that I want to drive everyone from you. I wanted to bring you close together—you and him. Speak to me. Speak out all your heart to me. What you feel and what you suffer.
>
> RICHARD: I am wounded, Bertha.
>
> BERTHA: How wounded, dear? Explain to me what you mean. I will try to understand everything you say. In what way are you wounded?
>
> RICHARD, *releases his hand and, taking her head between his hands, bends it back and gazes long into her eyes*: I have a deep, deep wound of doubt in my soul.
>
> BERTHA, *motionless*. Doubt of me?
>
> RICHARD: Yes.
>
> BERTHA: I am yours. *In a whisper*. If I died this moment, I am yours.
>
> RICHARD, *still gazing at her and speaking as if to an absent person*: I have wounded my soul for you— a deep wound of doubt which can never be healed. I can never know, never in this world. I do not wish to know or to believe. I do not care. It is not in the darkness of belief that I desire you. But in restless living wounding doubt. To hold you by no bonds, even of love, to be united with you in body and soul in utter nakedness—for this I longed. And now I am tired for a while, Bertha. My wound tires me. (p. 112)

As Richard's final speech, this must suggest what he has worked to achieve throughout the play. Right after it, *"he stretches himself out wearily along the lounge"* (p. 112). Under the circumstances, a "wounding doubt" has not been easily evoked. Sadomasochistic projects require considerable ingenuity and energy since they usually involve a progressive sophistication of pain. Each vicarious adventure quickly fades; ingenuity alone can improve upon preceding experience, as with the ancient debauchees in de Sade's books who evolve more and more complex erotic engineering to satisfy their wearying desires. Though they gradually become impotent, they never really give up.

In this context, Richard's "wounding doubt" appears a refinement of the sadomasochistic quests in *Dubliners*. The progression in *Dubliners* is to more sophisticated treatments of sadomasochism —from the bold threats of an old pervert in "An Encounter" to the aesthetic sadomasochism of Gabriel in "The Dead." But even Gabriel does not enjoy "wounding doubt," so much as the certain realization that Gretta once loved Michael Furey. Richard achieves not only a wounding doubt, but the bonus pleasure of Bertha's eager solicitude: "Forget me, Dick. Forget me and love me again as you did the first time. I want my lover. To meet him, to go to him, to give myself to him. You, Dick. O, my strange wild lover, come back to me again!" (p. 112).

In *Exiles*, Richard both avenges himself on his mother and satisfies her. His revenge is in proving to her spirit that he is above the Irish-Catholic moral code; his pleasing her is in having spoken with her voice and acted according to her spiritual instruction, thereby proving to her that she had been correct in opposing his liaison with Bertha. This dual satisfaction, revenge and fidelity, is in his voice in the final speech, where *"speaking as if to an absent person,"* he addresses not only Bertha but his mother as well: "I have wounded my soul for you—a deep wound of doubt which can never be healed" (p. 112).

Spiritually symbiotic with his mother, in wounding his own soul he has wounded her. Also, he has injured Bertha with whom he had longed "to be united . . . in body and soul in utter nakedness" (p. 112). His sadistic revenge and pleasure are more sophisticated than the crude physical injuries worked by Eugenie and her friends on Madame de Mistival in de Sade's *Philosophy in the Bedroom*. There, in ecstasy, Eugenie watches her mother violated by a syphilitic valet, then sent forth nude, her sexual organ sewn shut.[17]

Richard's masochism also surpasses the comic tortures achieved in Masoch's *Venus in Furs* by Severin, whose final abasement is to be whipped by his rival. This degrading satisfaction corresponds to Richard's more refined torment at the end of *Exiles*. He "witnesses" vicariously his own betrayal and he enjoys the possibility that Robert has beaten him. The refinement is that he visualizes an erotic betrayal he does not actually see, doubts whether it has really occurred, and is solaced in his ambiguity by Bertha.

Also, in *Exiles*, the experience of the female characters counterplots that of the men. Richard and Robert would come together through the common vessel, Bertha, as Joyce suggested in his notes: "The bodily possession of Bertha by Robert, repeated often, would certainly bring into almost carnal contact the two men. Do they desire this? To be united, that is carnally through the person and body of Bertha as they cannot, without dissatisfaction and degradation—be united carnally man to man as man to woman?" (p. 123). But Bertha and Beatrice would come together through the common vessel Richard. One significance of the uneasy encounter between the women in Act III is in the suggestion of lesbianism, in Bertha especially through an image of the eight-year epistolary affair between Richard and Beatrice. As a sketch of feminine sexual experience, Joyce's portrayal of Bertha predicts the insightful portraits of the inner imaginings of Gerty McDowell and Molly Bloom in

[17] Marquis de Sade, *Philosophy in the Bedroom* in *The Complete Justine, Philosophy in the Bedroom, and Other Writings* (New York, 1966), pp. 362–367.

Ulysses, as it is a further development of the studies in *Dubliners* of Eveline, Maria, Emily Sinico, and Gretta Conroy, Bertha's immediate predecessor.

Bertha's conversation with Beatrice turns at first on her assuming their common "intimacy" with Richard:

> BEATRICE: . . . If any change has come into [Richard's] life since he came back you must know and feel it.
> BERTHA: You could know it just as well. You are very intimate in this house.
> BEATRICE: I am not the only person who is intimate here. *They both look at each other coldly in silence for some moments. Bertha lays aside the paper and sits down on a chair nearer to Beatrice.*
> BERTHA, *placing her hand on Beatrice's knee*: So you also hate me, Miss Justice?
> BEATRICE, *with an effort*: Hate you? I?
> BERTHA, *insistently but softly*: Yes. You know what it means to hate a person?
> BEATRICE: Why should I hate you? I have never hated anyone.
> BERTHA: Have you never loved anyone? *She puts her hand on Beatrice's wrist.* Tell me. You have? (p. 97)

Notwithstanding Bertha's knowledge of the long correspondence between Beatrice and Richard, it turns out that the "other person" intimate with Richard is Robert Hand. But in the course of this exchange, Joyce suggests, chiefly through stage directions, Bertha's attraction for Beatrice. Taking her hands, Bertha precipitates an understandable nervousness in Beatrice:

> BERTHA, *going to her impulsively*: I am in such suffering. Excuse me if I was rude. I want us to be friends. *She holds out her hands.* Will you?
> BEATRICE, *taking her hands*: Gladly.
> BERTHA, *looking at her*: What lovely long eyelashes you have! And your eyes have such a sad expression!
> BEATRICE, *smiling*: I see very little with them. They are very weak.
> BERTHA, *warmly*: But beautiful. *She embraces her quietly and kisses her. Then withdraws from her a little shyly.* (p. 101)

At the conclusion of this scene, Bertha again takes Beatrice's hand and says:

> It is so strange that we spoke like this now. But I always wanted to. Did you?
>
> BEATRICE: I think I did, too.
>
> BERTHA, *smiling*: Even in Rome. When I went out for a walk with Archie I used to think about you, what you were like, because I knew about you from Dick. I used to look at different persons, coming out of churches or going by in carriages, and think that perhaps they were like you. Because Dick told me you were dark.
>
> BEATRICE, *again nervously*: Really?
>
> BERTHA, *pressing her hand*: Goodbye then—for the present. (pp. 101–102)

In notes which refer to Bertha, Joyce was somewhat more explicit about lesbianism. He explains two lists of words which associate with Bertha. The first refers to Christmas at Galway. A girl "thumps the piano and sits with her dark-complexioned gipsy-looking girl friend Emily Lyons on the window sill" (p. 121). Later, Emily leaves for America. Her friend "cries for the pain of separation and for the dangers of the sea" (p. 121). Emily becomes an image for the girl's own departing youth, and a "prophecy of a later dark male" (p. 122). The conclusion of Joyce's note sheds considerable light on the liaison between Bertha and Beatrice and its meaning in *Exiles*:

> A faint glimmer of lesbianism irradiates this mind. This girl [Emily] too is dark, even like a gypsy, and she too, like the dark lover who sleeps in Rahoon, is going away from her, the man-killer and perhaps also the love-killer, over the dark sea which is distance, the extinction of interest and death. They have no male lovers and are moved vaguely one towards the other, the friend is older, stronger, can travel alone, braver, a prophecy of a later dark male. The passiveness of her character to all that is not vital to its existence, and yet a passiveness which is suffused with tenderness. (p. 122)

As a gloss on the relationship between Bertha and Beatrice, this note deserves careful attention. If the "mind" Joyce describes refers to Bertha, Joyce has attributed to her an aggressive destructiveness. She is "the man-killer" and perhaps "the love-killer," fixed in a way reminiscent of Gretta in "The Dead" on "a dark lover who sleeps in Rahoon." Was she destructive to him as she is to his feminine counterpart, the "dark" gypsy-like Emily? The two women mentioned in Joyce's notes have "no male lovers," and are "moved vaguely one towards the other." Though the Bertha figure is aggressively destructive, her dark-haired friend, like Beatrice Justice, is older, stronger, braver. These attributes notwithstanding, she is not imagined as aggressively destructive, but as passively tender. In this strange alliance, the Bertha figures appears sadistic, Beatrice masochistic. As a gloss on *Exiles*, Joyce's note suggests that Bertha and Beatrice engage in the usual sadomasochistic *pas de deux* practiced more elaborately by a series of Joyce's male partners, of whom Richard and Robert are perhaps the most obvious examples. The feminine relationship constitutes a subplot, stemming from Joyce's instinctive sense of dramatic counterpoint, and from his preoccupation with *liaisons dangereuses*.

In *Giacomo Joyce*, Joyce devoted further attention to a figure shrewdly imagined as a *femme fatale*. Here, the object of his attention seemed a combination of Bertha and Beatrice, her "pale face surrounded by heavy odorous furs. Her movements are shy and nervous."[18] Throughout *Giacomo Joyce*, the narrator perceives the young woman in images of alluring if hazardous animality. Even her handwriting is "cob-web" (*Giacomo Joyce*, p. 1), the edges of her gown "web-soft," her stocking, "a leg-stretched web" (*Giacomo Joyce*, p. 9). Her lips are "long lewdly leering"; they are "dark-blooded molluscs" (*Giacomo Joyce*, p. 5). She reveals a "lithe smooth naked body shimmering with silver scales" (*Giacomo Joyce*, p. 7). As she walks, her hair "slowly uncoils and falls." Her dark, suffering eyes are "beautiful as the eyes of an antelope," her speech after an operation, that of "a bird twittering after storm"

[18] James Joyce, *Giacomo Joyce*, Richard Ellmann, ed. (New York, 1968), p. 1. Subsequent references to *Giacomo Joyce* in parentheses are to this edition.

(*Giacomo Joyce*, p. 11), her voice to Mamma that of a frightened pullet (*Giacomo Joyce*, p. 12). Eventually, she becomes a deadly snake: "She coils towards me along the crumpled lounge. I cannot move or speak. Coiling approach of starborn flesh. Adultery of wisdom. No. I will go. I will. —Jim, love! Soft sucking lips kiss my left armpit: a coiling kiss on myriad veins. I burn! I crumple like a burning leaf! From my right armpit a fang of flame leaps out. A starry snake has kissed me: a cold night-snake. I am lost!" (*Giacomo Joyce*, p. 15). In her velvet iris a "burning needleprick stings and quivers" (*Giacomo Joyce*, p. 1). Her face is fascinating and revolting, a study in decadence: "Shadows streak her falsely smiling face, smitten by the hot creamy light, grey wheyhued shadows under the jawbones, streaks of eggyolk yellow on the moistened brow, rancid yellow humour lurking within the softened pulp of her eyes" (*Giacomo Joyce*, p. 2). Later, she greets him "wintrily and passes up the stair case darting at me for an instant out of her sluggish sidelong eyes a jet of liquorish venom" (*Giacomo Joyce*, p. 15). Throughout this extraordinary document, the woman, however alluring, has been pictured as deadly and destructive. One cannot be sure of a direct connection between the depiction of Bertha and Beatrice and the depiction of a woman in *Giacomo Joyce*, though *Exiles* was on his mind at about the same time as the events depicted in *Giacomo Joyce*.[19] Richard Ellmann remarks, "Joyce was not the man to repeat himself, so it seems probable that at some time before mid-November of 1914 he had decided to pillage rather than to publish *Giacomo Joyce*. He did so not only for the sake of *A Portrait* but also for *Ulysses* and for his play *Exiles*."[20] Ellmann does not say what Joyce pillaged from *Giacomo Joyce* to enrich *Exiles*, but certainly in their combination of dark destructiveness and ten-

[19] "It would appear that the events and moods collocated in *Giacomo Joyce* took place between late 1911 and the middle of 1914. While Joyce probably relied to some extent on earlier notes, he could not have written it down as a whole before the end of June 1914." Richard Ellmann, introduction to *Giacomo Joyce*, p. xv.

[20] *Ibid.*, p. xvi.

der passivity, in their mutual exoticism, in their ambiguous attraction for an exiled Irishman, Bertha-Beatrice resemble the composite woman in *Giacomo Joyce*. They also fit what Stanislaus Joyce referred to as his brother's "Iago complex," that women were the *radix malorum*, a view further suggested by the permeation of *Exiles* with the deathly iciness of Richard's mother, which might well correspond to the erotic iciness implicit in the Bertha-Beatrice alliance.

After the explications of sadomasochistic project in *Exiles*, it might seem perverse to affirm that after all Joyce's cryptic play is a comedy of humours, permeated more by a tone of sardonic amusement than of high seriousness. Had Joyce followed the model of Ibsen in theme and tone as well as in structure and theatrical trapping,[21] we might have had a highly serious exploration of contemporary ethic which could have ended like *Hedda Gabbler* on a tragic, or at least on a melodramatic note. One of the earliest readers, Ezra Pound, wrote Joyce that, "if there were an Ibsen theatre in full blast I dare say your play could go into it."[22]

Perhaps because he took it, not without reason, as an Ibsen-like play, Pound's further remarks on *Exiles* bear consideration here. They establish the impression *Exiles* would have made on the Ibsen-conditioned consciousness. In his essay on "Mr. James Joyce and the Modern Stage," Pound castigates contemporary theatre, particularly Shaw ("the intellectualized cheese-mite") for "trivialized Ibsen":[23] that is, in Shaw, "Ibsen with the sombre reality taken out, a little Nietzsche put in to enliven things, and a technique of dialogue superadded from Wilde."[24] Though Pound objected to

---

[21] Here, I assume what may be invalid, that the overall spirit in Ibsen is serious. His tone may also be sardonic, thus closer to the spirit in Joyce than I have said. Certainly, in tone and theme the later Ibsen, particularly of *When We Dead Awaken*, resembles Joyce. But to critics like Pound and probably to most audiences it was not obvious that Ibsen was not entirely serious, especially in middle plays like *An Enemy of the People* and *Hedda Gabbler*.

[22] Pound to Joyce, 6–12 September 1915, *Pound/Joyce*, p. 47.

[23] *Ibid.*, p. 51.

[24] *Ibid.*

Exiles as "unstageable," he did not question its stageability on the grounds it was a bad play:

> It is distinctly a play. It has the form of a play . . . an inner form . . .
> the acts and speeches of one person work into the acts and speeches
> of another and make the play into an indivisible, integral whole.
> The action takes place in less than twenty-four hours, in two rooms,
> both near Dublin, so that even the classical unities are uninjured.
> It could not . . . be anything but a play. And yet it is absolutely unfit
> for the stage as we know it. It is dramatic. Strong, well-wrought sen-
> tences flash from the speech and give it "dramatic edge" such as we
> have in Ibsen, when some character comes out with, "There is no
> mediator between God and man"; I mean sentences dealing with
> fundamentals.[25]

For Pound, the problem with *Exiles* was not in the play but with prospective audiences: "The trouble with Mr. Joyce's play is precisely that he *is* at prise with reality. It is a 'dangerous' play precisely because the author is portraying an intellectual-emotional struggle, because he is dealing with actual thought, actual questioning, not with cliches of thought and emotion. . . . It is untheatrical, or unstageable, precisely because the closeness and cogency of the process is, I think, too great for an audience to be able to follow . . . under present conditions."[26] And yet, Pound reasoned that the "actual thought, actual questioning in *Exiles*," too great for an audience to follow, had to do with what I have previously described as rationalizations of Richard's quest in *Exiles*: "[Joyce] is actually driving in the mind upon the age-long problems of the rights of personality and of the responsibility of the intelligent individual for the conduct of those about him, upon the age-long question of the relative rights of intellect, and emotion, and sensation, and sentiment."[27] As Samuel Beckett wrote in *Endgame*: "The old questions, the old answers. There's nothing like them."

[25] *Ibid.*, p. 50.
[26] *Ibid.*, p. 52.
[27] *Ibid.*, p. 56.

Pound attributes a rather more solemn intent to *Exiles* than Joyce, an eternal comic, perhaps even cynic, may have intended. But if *Exiles* proves less serious than Pound thought, it is not trivial—not either Shavian or Wildean. It is a comedy without conventional amusement, but with a black laughter that was ahead of its time. Therefore, Pound was correct in saying that audiences were not *yet* ready for *Exiles*. We have since grown accustomed to the savage humor of theatre of cruelty, of which *Exiles* portends, in theme and tone if not in technique and structure.

In a recent essay, David Hayman has even perceived farcical elements in *Exiles* which, with one exception (the character of Robert Hand) escaped Pound.[28] Though Hayman goes too far in calling *Exiles* "a bedroom farce," his perception may be closer to the Joycean mode than Pound's rather more grave perception. Hayman feels that Joyce "soberly approaches the more conventionally comic in *Exiles*":

> Adultery, both physical and spiritual, is the focus of the play's many themes. It is taken seriously, but Joyce was aware of its traditionally comic function as he was of what he called the "modern" tendency to divert the audience's sympathy from the "fancyman" to the cuckhold. Already in the notebook for *Exiles* the male principals resemble the traditional comic opponents, the volatile trickster who takes advantage of social complacency and the passive victim rendered vulnerable by his refusal or inability to conform to the surface mores of society. If Joyce fulfills his aim to revitalize the relationship by reversing our sympathies, his success is due in large measure to the retention of some of the traditional qualities of both stereotypes . . . fallen angel and risen demon, Lucifer and Mephistopheles, or Pierrot and Harlequin, Richard and Robert are capitalizing on their disabilities in true clown fashion.[29]

Professor Hayman's opinion is within the context of an admirable

---

[28] Pound noted "the exquisite picture of Robert squirting his perfume pump." Pound to Joyce, 6–12 September 1915, *Pound/Joyce*, p. 47.

[29] David Hayman, "Forms of Folly in Joyce: A Study of Clowning in *Ulysses*," *ELH* 34, no. 2 (June, 1967): 262.

effort to define the "forms of folly"—the farcical mode—throughout Joyce, and throughout modern literature. His overall explanation is eminently valuable and useful, but in discussing *Exiles* he may have had to stretch a point to make one. "Played broadly," as he suggests the play be produced, *Exiles* could indeed be farcical, though such might be true of many serious plays. Certainly, it is not obvious either from the text of *Exiles* or from Joyce's notes that he thought of the play as a bedroom farce. What is clearer is Joyce taking his usual mischievous amusement in the plight of his characters while at the same time another aspect of his personality took them seriously. The incongruity in *Exiles* between a quixotically ridiculous quest for neurotic vicarious experience, and the high seriousness of the more "intellectual" dialogue accounts for some of the amusement the play may yield. But this amusement does not strike me as essentially farcical, however much it may approach farce on the scale of our response to humor.

If David Hayman goes too far in describing *Exiles* as a farce, Ezra Pound had gone to the other extreme in dwelling on its serious intent. With Joyce, the truth usually lies somewhere in between. The problem remains to describe *Exiles* as a comedy in a uniquely Joycean mode. Northrop Frye's theory of comedy—particularly what he says about comedy of humours—will be useful here.

In the simplest formulation of comic structure, "a young man wants a young woman . . . his desire is resisted by some opposition, usually paternal . . . near the end of the play some twist in the plot enables the hero to have his will."[30] It is enlightening to assume for now that *Exiles* proceeds upon a similar formula. Richard wants Bertha. His mother has opposed this desire. He overcomes this opposition and "has his will." Though the explication of sado-masochistic quest in *Exiles* demonstrates the inadequacy of this simple formula for a play so complicated, the formula cannot be put aside completely. Richard does "want" Bertha, his comic bride.

[30] Northrop Frye, *Anatomy of Criticism* (Princeton, 1957), p. 163.

Obviously, he had achieved a comic triumph nine years earlier. But there is a sense in which he once again triumphs in the present of the play. The context in which he wishes to "have" Bertha differs chiefly in detail from an archetypal comedy which traditionally ends with a marriage feast, and has involved the overcoming of parental opposition. As Frye perceives, the hero overcomes parental opposition often by incorporating the antagonist into the "new society" at play's end.[31] Even this is true of *Exiles*. The "new society" is in Richard's imagination, which teems with couplings he vicariously enjoys. Among these is the spiritual unison with his dead mother, along with a considerably altered but nonetheless conclusive liaison with Bertha. Thus he neurotically incorporates the opposing parent into his new society.

In addition, through the medium of Bertha as common vessel, he has united himself vicariously with Robert Hand. Furthermore, the "counterplot" which centers on the lesbian connections between Bertha and Beatrice brings them together with Richard as *their* common vessel. The wedding festivity at the end of *Exiles* occurs chiefly in Richard's imagination, where a spintrian liaison contorts, presided over by the stern ghost of Mrs. Rowan. It would be difficult to find a more intricate fulfillment of the simple comic formula Frye describes.

In March 1903, Joyce had predicted to his mother that he would write a comedy in about nine years.[32] According to Richard Ellmann, shortly before this assertion, Joyce had spent his days in Paris reading Ben Jonson, "studying both plays and poems to improve his own technique."[33] Though Joyce carefully studied Jon-

---

[31] "The tendency of comedy is to include as many people as possible in its final society: the blocking characters are more often reconciled or converted than simply repudiated." *Ibid.*, p. 165.

[32] "My book of songs will be published in the spring of 1907. My first comedy about five years later." Joyce to Mrs. John Stanislaus Joyce, 20 March 1903, *Letters*, vol. 2, p. 38. Since *Exiles* was published in 1914, Joyce was off in his prediction by only two years—assuming that *Exiles* was the comedy he prophesied.

[33] Richard Ellmann, *James Joyce* (New York, 1959), p. 124.

son's plays, a direct influence on *Exiles* of the Jonsonian comedy of humours cannot be established. The protestant moral vision underlying Jonson's comedy[34] would differ radically in any case from that of Joyce, whose vision in its origin was a combination of the medieval and the Irish-Catholic.[35]

Obviously, the dramatic techniques in *Exiles* owe far more to Ibsen than to any other playwright. We are left with the observation that Joyce read Jonson's comedies at about the time he predicted a comedy of his own, that he may have written *Exiles* to fulfill his own prediction, and that his vision became progressively more comic, as in *Dubliners*. But, in addition, *Exiles* both verifies and complicates Northrop Frye's description of the comedy of humours, in which "the humour's dramatic function is to express a state of what might be called ritual bondage. He is obsessed by his humour and his function in the play is primarily to repeat his obsession."[36] Bound to his mother and to the sadomasochistic project they mutually engender, Richard functions dramatically as a humour who both manipulates and obstructs the other characters. But he must also be a comic hero within the simple formula used earlier and in the struggle to reject his bondage. Confirming his bondage and rejecting it, Richard emerges enslaved and liberated.

But there is another form of bondage which confirms him as a comic hero. Dublin's behavior is circumscribed by an Irish-Catholic-bourgeois moral code based on the right of mutual possession by husband and wife. Though Richard's struggle against this bondage provides the rationalization for his sadomasochistic project, he denies its application to his own affairs: "Who am I that I should call myself master of your heart or of any woman's? Bertha, love him,

[34] See James D. Redwine, Jr., "Beyond Psychology: The Moral Basis of Jonson's Theory of Humour Characterization," *ELH* 28, no. 3 (September, 1961): 316–334.

[35] "[Joyce's] whole mind showed the mental and moral training of the Church." Mary and Padraic Colum, *Our Friend James Joyce* (New York, 1958), p. 135. This has been gone into at such length by various scholars, such as Noon and Sullivan, that I see no point in belaboring it.

[36] Frye, *Anatomy*, p. 168.

be his, give yourself to him if you desire—or if you can" (p. 75). Richard is both a comic hero and a culture hero whose *non-serviams* prepare for a utopian society which would challenge the control of erotic experience by conventional society. In *Exiles* Joyce asserts and parodies the erotic utopias which have been the stock in trade of sadomasochistic literature since de Sade's cunningly equipped castle set off from the world of conventional experience,[37] or Masoch's Carpathian mansion simmering in a Central European backwood spa.

The scene of past orgies and present assignations, Robert Hand's cottage at Ranelagh is both an image of comic freedom from Dublin's severe regulation of sexual mores, and what Frye calls the "sham utopia," often found in comedy of humours: "a society of ritual bondage constructed by an act of humourous or pedantic will, like the academic retreat in *Love's Labor's Lost*."[38] Created more out of whimsey than erotic efficiency—the special perfections of de Sade and Masoch—the operations room in Robert's cottage, Joyce describes at the beginning of Act II:

> On the right, forward, a small black piano, on the rest of which is an open piece of music. Farther back a door leading to the street door. In the wall, at the back, folding doors, draped with dark curtains, leading to a bedroom. Near the piano a large table, on which is a tall oil lamp with a wide yellow shade. Chairs, upholstered, near this table. A small cardtable more forward. Against the back wall a bookcase. In the left wall, back, a window looking out into the garden, and, forward, a door and porch, also leading to the garden. Easychairs here and there. Plants in the porch and near the draped folding doors. On the walls are many framed black and white designs. In the right corner, back, a sideboard; and in

[37] A place of incredible debaucheries, Durcet's chateau in *The 120 Days of Sodom* is impossibly inaccessible. A bridge over a thousand foot precipice once removed or destroyed, "there is not on this earth a single being, of no matter what species you may imagine, capable of gaining a small plot of level land." Marquis de Sade, *The 120 Days of Sodom and Other Writings* (New York, 1967), pp. 236–237.

[38] Frye, *Anatomy*, p. 169.

the centre of the room, left of the table, a group consisting of a standing Turkish pipe, a low oil stove, which is not lit, and a rocking chair. It is the evening of the same day. (p. 57)

It is the kind of room into which a girl might be invited for a look at the "framed black and white designs" on the wall, and where she might be conscious of the arty exoticism of "a standing turkish pipe." These details and the subsequent description of Robert Hand, preparing for his conquest of Bertha, Ezra Pound thought the most amusing and stageable in the play. The stage directions read:

> ROBERT HAND, in evening dress, is seated at the piano. The candles are not lit but the lamp on the table is lit. He plays softly in the bass the first bars of Wolfram's song in the last act of "Tannhäuser." Then he breaks off and, resting an elbow on the ledge of the keyboard, meditates. Then he rises and, pulling a pump from behind the piano, walks here and there in the room ejecting from it into the air sprays of perfume. He inhales the air slowly and then puts the pump back behind the piano. He sits down on a chair near the table, and smoothing his hair carefully, sighs once or twice. Then, thrusting his hands into his trousers pockets, he leans back, stretches out his legs, and waits. A knock is heard at the street door. He rises quickly. (pp. 57–58)

What Pound described as "the exquisite picture of Robert squirting his perfume pump,"[39] hints at Joyce's evaulation of this sexual utopia as a sham, the stage setting for Robert's heavy-handed Don Gioviannism, as it had been years before also for Richard's rather more somber debaucheries.[40] Even those had about them the air of professorial experimentation, the operation of Richard's pedantic will as a counterpoint to the clumsy vulgarity of Robert Hand. Describing their earlier use of this cottage, Robert remembers the pleasure, Richard the experiment:

[39] Pound, *Pound/Joyce*, p. 47.
[40] Hugh Kenner refers to Joyce's explicit repudiation in *Exiles* of "the Norwegian's [i.e. Ibsen] Utopia-at-the-other-side-of-free-love." Kenner, "Joyce's *Exiles*," p. 389.

ROBERT: . . . Lord, when I think of our wild nights long ago—talks
by the hour, plans, carouses, revelry . . .

RICHARD: In our house.

ROBERT: It is mine now. I have kept it ever since though I don't go
there often. Whenever you like to come let me know. You must
come some night. It will be old times again. *He lifts his glass, and
drinks.* Prosit!

RICHARD: It was not only a house of revelry; it was to be the hearth
of a new life. *Musing.* And in that name all our sins were committed. (pp. 40–41)

Psychologically, Richard's pedantic will is a function of sadomasochistic neurosis; dramatically, it is a function of his obsessive humour. In *Exiles* these are identical. Thus, the "action" of *Exiles*,
Richard's quest for vicarious experience at the behest and in spite
of his dead mother, is also the action of a humour who, in Frye's
terms, "is able to force much of the play's society into line with his
obsession."[41] In psychoanalytic terms, Richard's obsession is a repetition compulsion stressed by Stekel as common to all sadomasochistic neuroses. Compelled to reenact the scenes which trouble his
imagination, he must force himself and all the other characters in
the play to play predetermined roles. Dramatically, this compulsion
to repeat is identical to a governing principle of comedy of humours, "that unincremental repetition, the literary imitation of
ritual bondage, is funny."[42] David Hayman's perception is close to
this when he notices in *Exiles* Joyce's approximation to the Berg-
sonian view "of the comic man as a machine."[43] Described in Joyce's
notes as an "automystic" (Notes to *Exiles*, p. 113), Richard amuses
in that he is the slave to a form of ritual bondage to his mother and
to the past which forces him into obsessive repetition. In this sense
like the typical Dubliner he is a mechanical man, as bound to past
patterns as Patrick Morkan's horse in "The Dead," which was
obliged to reenact his everyday treadmill existence even when for a

41 Frye, *Anatomy*, p. 169.
42 *Ibid.*, p. 168.
43 Hayman, "Forms of Folly in Joyce," p. 262.

Sunday he was ridden through the park. In drama as in life, the compulsion to repeat is often the compulsion to reenact. Life becomes theater because it has been so from the first instant of wish to stage scenes contradicted by reality. As Stekel points out, the neurotic is both actor and spectator in a scene he once witnessed as a drama and has since embroidered. Unless released by therapy or death from his ritual bondage, the sadomasochist must stage progressively more enslaving scenes. His ultimate neurotic wish will often be a variation of Severin's in *Venus in Furs*. Ritual bondage becomes concretely realized through the imagery of imprisonment: the quintessential torment is to be tied and beaten, hence the preponderance of chains and locks, ropes and whips in sadomasochistic pornography. *Exiles* is not pornographic, but the psychological patterns of deviant pornography are there. By the highly theatrical *Circe* episode in *Ulysses*, the sadomasochistic ritual bondage of Leopold Bloom of whom Richard is a portent will become concrete, and Joyce will employ the imagery of pornography to express it. In *Exiles*, part of Richard's quest has been to throw off the bondage of conventional morality. Thus at the end he says to Bertha that he wished "to hold you by no bonds" (p. 112). He himself prefers the subtler confinement of "wounding doubt," which would henceforth inhibit his response to her more effectively than real chains, and would at the same time allow his response to her to be the enactment of his compulsive need for betrayal, one of Joyce's recurrent motifs. The rejection of conventional bonds—marriage, friendship, loyalty—all of which require betrayal, is so important a theme in *Exiles* that Richard must put it in the form of a parody of Christianity. As he says to Robert in the first act: "There is a faith still stranger than the faith of the disciple in his master . . . The faith of a master in the disciple who will betray him" (p. 44).

In *Anatomy of Criticism*, Northrop Frye recognizes a similarity between the action of conventional comedy and that of psychoanalytic procedure. The total mythos of comedy, implies "a stable and harmonious order disrupted by folly, obsession, forgetfulness, 'pride and prejudice,' or events not understood by the characters themselves, and then restored." "Ritually," Frye says, "this ternary action is . . . like a contest of summer and winter in which winter occupies the middle action; psychologically, it is like the removal of a neurosis or blocking point and the restoration of an unbroken current of energy and memory."[44] This ternary structure is not ordinarily present in a play, but it is usually implied. In *Exiles*, however, there was never a "golden age," only the neurotic family structure of "smiling handsome father," "cold-hearted mother," and Richard, caught in the middle, preferring his sunny father but finally conforming to his spooky mother. The third part of this ternary structure is implied in Richard's sad, Ibsenian wish to kindle the joy of life in "the hearth of a new life." However, *Exiles* remains in the ironic mode because the new life turns out to be a sham utopia, teeming in Richard's imagination, parodied by the sex-nest in Ranelagh. Psychologically, the play does not lead to the removal of "a neurosis or a blocking point," and thus there is not in *Exiles* "the restoration of an unbroken current of energy and memory" (p. 171). At the end of the play, bereft of energy, Richard "stretches himself out wearily along the lounge" (p. 112). Memory is only more deeply repressed.

[44] Frye, *Anatomy*, p. 171.

CONCLUSION

A Portrait of the Artist as a Young Man and *Ulysses*

"I could see him vividly, half-drunk on words and full of contempt and exaltation, pacing before the blackboard chalked with quotations from Joyce and Yeats and Sean O'Casey; thin, nervous, neat, pacing as though he walked a high wire of meaning upon which no one of us would ever dare venture. I could hear him: "Stephen's problem, like ours, was not actually one of creating the uncreated conscience of his race, but of creating the *uncreated features of his face*." Ralph Ellison, *Invisible Man*, p. 307.

One could not expect a theme so pervasive as Dublin's habitual sadomasochism to disappear from Joyce's later work. In fact, throughout this study I have suggested that *A Portrait of the Artist* and *Ulysses* move towards resolutions of the paralytic complexity delineated in *Dubliners* and *Exiles*. Though in his later work Joyce does not restrict himself to therapy, a cure was of pressing importance for him. Notwithstanding his rejection of conventional heroism,[1] and his occasional aversion for the Dubliners, Joyce seldom perceived himself as an artist apart from some consideration of his obligation to them. This consideration does not necessarily imply a political or social conscience, but it does imply a moral and psychological conscience, reflected in Stephen Dedalus's final resolve in *A Portrait*: "I go to encounter for the millionth time the reality of experience and to forge in the smithy of my soul the uncreated

[1] See footnote 27 in the Introduction of this study.

conscience of my race" (p. 253). Throughout the foregoing chapters I have stressed that in Dublin, the "reality of experience" was consistently evaded, by largely unconscious communion with the experience of others, usually to acquire a power which had been lost in the nightmare of personal and political history. This contrivance of power must enter the Dubliners then as fiction, pathologically distorted, illusory. Alone among his compatriots, Joyce's Stephen braves contact with "real" power, and in Joyce's mind, actual power grew out of courageous encounter with "the reality of experience."

For such an encounter, *A Portrait* conditions the artist-hero. *Ulysses* is the encounter, a delicate subversion of the repressive fictions in Dublin. One must inspect *Ulysses* as an "encounter with the real," on the assumption that this encounter was meant to correct the adroit evasions of his earlier characters. But one must keep in mind that this encounter is itself a forgery, implied in Stephen's choice of the double-meaning verb. For therapeutic ends he must counterfeit at the same time as he must create a thing of lasting value out of strong and harshly tempered material. So close to real coin, the ambiguous forgery of *Ulysses* rings true alongside the debased currency of human rapport in Dublin, the constant betrayal which served as a medium for exchange of contempt. Nevertheless, Joyce was not completely successful in imaginatively dissolving Dublin's sadomasochistic temperament, even by means of an aesthetic transubstantiation of experience. Therefore, one must deal scrupulously with the Stephen Dedalus and particularly with the Leopold Bloom of *Ulysses*.

In *A Portrait*, Stephen desperately struggled to see through and reject an inclination to punish himself by imaginative projection into roles which went against his grain, in Dublin a typical masochistic submission clearly shown, as we have seen, in the story "Eveline." Stephen's strong rejection of submissive roles dictated by a culture he comes to despise is a prerequisite for his role as culture hero. For such a role the characters in *Dubliners* had been poorly equipped. Even Richard Rowan in *Exiles*, despite strength and intelligence, desired chiefly vicarious adventure, second-hand erotic action.

The nets of Ireland confine the Dubliners to a script devised by some other person or institution. Of course, as I have demonstrated earlier, each Dubliner contrives his own manipulative use of this condition of habitual servitude, but Stephen alone continually discards the scripts he has been handed. The role of dutiful son he rejects, to Simon's dismay; the role of docile student he refuses, to the bewilderment of teachers and peers. Most significantly, he even turns away from the role of humble priest, most alluring of all because most publicly submissive and most mysteriously powerful. He will not display himself in clerical gesture before the world, though he had vividly lived such a role over and over in his head: "In that dim life which he had lived through in his musings he had assumed the voices and gestures which he noted with various priests. He had bent his knee sideways like such a one, he had shaken the thurible only slightly like such a one, his chasuble had swung open like that of such another" (p. 158). But his self-image gradually dims in such a role, and when he thinks of himself in community with other Jesuits, the process of rejection appears irreversible: "Some instinct . . . stronger than education or piety, quickened within him at every near approach to that life . . . and armed him against acquiescence" (p. 161). The final stage of his aversion for the role of Catholic priest arrives when he cannot allow his own features to dissolve in the "undefined face" of the universal Jesuit: "The colour faded and became strong like a changing glow of pallid red brick. Was it the raw reddish glow he had so often seen on wintry mornings on the shaven gills of the priests? The face was eyeless and sour-favoured and devout, shot with pink tinges of suffocated anger. Was it not a mental spectre of the face of one of the jesuits whom some of the boys called Lantern Jaws and others Foxy Campbell?" (p. 161). Firmly established in the quest for his own as yet unclearly defined face, Stephen cannot allow the dissolution of his self-image into an "eyeless" impersonality. This stage of self-assertion, just prior to his actual discovery of a vocation, grew out of a gradual reaction against the process of repression he had experienced with memorable intensity during the retreat. Seldom in literature have the actual mechanics of repression been described so precisely. Father Arnall had used the Spiritual Exercises to usurp by terror Stephen's internal senses.[2] This procedure succeeds exactly at the point when, the sermons over, Stephen is alone in his room:

> The leprous company of his sins closed about him, breathing upon him, bending over him from all sides. He strove to forget them in an act of prayer, huddling his limbs closer together and binding down his eyelids: but the senses of his soul would not be bound and, though his eyes were shut fast, he saw the places where he had sinned and, though his ears were tightly covered, he heard. He desired with all his will not to hear or see. He desired till his frame shook under the strain of his desire and until the senses of his soul closed. They closed for an instant and then opened. He saw.
>
> A field of stiff weeds and thistles and tufted nettlebushes. Thick among the tufts of rank stiff growth lay battered canisters and clots and coils of solid excrement. A faint marshlight struggled upwards from all the ordure. (p. 137)

The "senses of his soul" compose an internal community mediating between the spirit and the world of perception. Father Arnall's threats had been leveled at the capitulation of this internal community. Though Stephen closed his external senses, eyes and ears, to the recall of sexual experience, though he closed his body to memory ("huddling his limbs close together"), he will not reject the pleasure of experience, thus submitting to Father Arnall's as-

---

[2] James R. Thrane has demonstrated the extent to which Father Arnall's sermons derive from *Hell Open to Christians, To Caution Them From Entering It*, the interpretation of Ignatius on hell by an Italian Jesuit, Giovanni Pietro Pinanonti. "Joyce's Sermon on Hell: Its Source and Backgrounds" in *A James Joyce Miscellany*, third series, ed. Marvin Magalaner (Carbondale, 1962), pp. 33–78.

sault on self, until that moment when the senses of his own soul close. At this point, Father Arnall has gotten inside him and pulled a closely guarded lever of self. When these internal senses open, Stephen's self-cession is complete. What he had persisted in seeing as attractive he now perceives as repulsive. Stephen's encounter with the reality of sensual experience has been internalized and converted to excrement.

We realize that Father Arnall's *coup d'etat* is not final. Stephen eventually pries the clerical hand away from a most intimate lever of self, and he will return to a newly ethereal perception of eros as the senses of his soul return to his own supervision. The famous vision of the girl on the beach is first external then internal. Now an artist-priest, Stephen has gone Father Arnall one better in power, thus recapturing his own internal senses: "He closed his eyes in the languor of sleep. His eyelids trembled as if they felt the vast cyclic movement of the earth and her watchers, trembled as if they felt the strange light of some new world" (p. 172). The "faint marshlight" of that excremental vision inspired by Father Arnall, has been replaced by "the strange light of some new world." Once again internalized, an encounter with external reality undergoes re-conversion: from excrement to light.

Nevertheless, the fifth chapter of *A Portrait* dramatizes the impermanence of even a primarily aesthetic posture. For such a posture does not permit Stephen to come to terms with his own humanity, much less with that of his family and friends. During his final encounter with Emma he turns off the valve of overt hostility, and opens "the spiritual-heroic refrigerating apparatus, invented and patented in all countries by Dante Alighieri."[3] I take this to mean that in view of his own misogyny—part of his pervasive contempt for Dublin—Stephen must employ the aesthetic role to

[3] For an extensive discussion of Stephen's relation to Emma, see my essay, "Stephen's Aesthetic in *A Portrait of the Artist*" in *The Celtic Cross*, ed. Ray Browne, William Roscelli, and Richard Loftus (West Lafayette, Ind., 1964), pp. 11–21.

cope with his neurotic responses. This role allows him to anesthetize himself, but it does not allow him to come to terms with his contempt. As long as he can only cope by means of a pose, he will still be following the pattern he has rejected in his Dubliners: that is, the reluctance to be freely human, the preference for artificial postures. He has put on the antic disposition of the manipulative neurotic by way of escaping the antic dispositions which pass for human life in Dublin.

When the chastened Stephen reappears in *Ulysses*, we sense his deliberate wish to free himself from imposture, in this case from the role of dandified artist: "My latin quarter hat. God, we simply must dress the character. I want puce gloves" (p. 42). When he no longer can remain at ease in the *role* of artist, according to someone else's script (Dante, Baudelaire, Nietzsche, Pater, or whoever), he can begin to be human. He can permit the exorcism of his own hatred for Dublin's matriarchal imperium, and reject the need to experience life as the projection of self into manufactured roles. When he says *"Non Serviam,"* he is refusing to assume a posture, which is to say that he can now be an artist without pretending to be one. For he had imagined his time in Paris as a theatrical phase: "You bowed to yourself in the mirror, stepping forward to applause earnestly, striking face. Hurray for the God-damned idiot! Hray!" (p. 41). He will be able to laugh at himself in this way once he is on the way to liberation from the repressive maternal image. He must shatter and re-create the "unsubstantial image his soul constantly beheld."

In "The Dead," Joyce hinted at Gabriel Conroy's ambivalent acquiescence in the influence of his mother's ghost—one of the living dead constituting a mythological community infesting the subconscious of Dublin. More openly than the other stories (except, perhaps, "Eveline") "The Dead" implied that an unconscious allegiance to the autocratic dead accounted for the pathology Joyce laid bare. *Exiles* dramatized this theme much more explicitly. Joyce merged a shrewd sense of the influence on present behavior of repressed neurotic loyalty with a vestigial sense of demonic spirituality.

The Joycean version of unconscious repression resembled that of Freud, for whom much of the unconscious was a malign realm, echoing with childhood injunctions long since barred from consciousness. As with Joyce's Dubliners, these injunctions were for the sake of banishing various instinctual drives from their legitimate operation. As a consequence, the repressed instincts ramified "like a fungus in the dark."[4] When Joyce comes to depict repressions explicitly emerging in *Ulysses,* he displays a similar sense of the unconscious as a moldy cellar. He added to this sense of the demonic unconscious a notion of its liaison with an impalpable region where "vast hosts of the dead" still maintained "their wayward and flickering existence" (*Dubliners,* p. 223). Joyce combined a rationalism like that of Freud with a Catholic sense of the reality of a spiritual world. This is not a place to enter the discussion of whether or not Joyce himself was a believer. It is enough to realize that his Dubliners believed, in the "narrow sense of the word" described by Haines in his condescending interrogation of Stephen in the "Telemachus" episode of *Ulysses.*

In *Ulysses,* Stephen confronts the demonic unconscious which had plagued his fictional predecessors. Haunted throughout by his mother's ghost, he refuses finally to acquiesce in the allegiance she demands.[5] Though it requires some effort to see in "The Dead"

---

[4] Sigmund Freud, "Repression" in *Collected Papers,* vol. 4, translated under the supervision of Joan Riviere (New York, 1959), p. 87.

[5] William Wasserstrom observes, "Plagued by conscience and sterilized by guilt, believing that he not cancer killed his mother, not her flesh but her spirit, he arrives in night-town. And in that desperate, frenzied, moment when he pleads with his mother's spirit to give him the word which will allow his own *logos* to form, help him to overcome the 'pectoral trauma' and deliver, transmute 'the daily bread of experience into the radiant body of everliving life'— in that instant he is told again, repent. This is the teaching of an exhausted whoredom and Stephen has no choice but to destroy his mother, the whore of Christ." "In Gertrude's Closet: Incest-Patterns in Recent Literature" in *Hidden Patterns: Studies in Psychoanalytic Literary Criticism,* ed. Leonard and Eleanor Manheim (New York, 1966), p. 287.

and in *Exiles* the theme of ghostly maternal imperium, Joyce could hardly have presented it more explicitly than in *Ulysses*. The dead mother is a constant presence whom Stephen first recalls early in "Telemachus": "Silently, in a dream she had come to him after her death, her wasted body within its loose brown graveclothes giving off an odour of wax and rosewood, her breath, that had bent upon him, mute, reproachful, a faint odour of wetted ashes" (p. 7). Until her exorcism in "Circe," she is seldom far from Stephen's thought, even though at times he imagines her in surrogate forms, as in his reflections on maternal love in "Nestor," or his documentation of the role of feminine domination in Shakespeare's life and art, in "Scylla and Charybdis."

But it is in "Circe" that Stephen must finally either destroy or acquiesce in her ghostly imperium. He does not resort in the end to the sadomasochistic subterfuges of Gabriel or Richard Rowan, who ambivalently defeat *and* succumb to their deathly mothers.

In "Circe," the brothel gas jet forecasts the eventual apparition of the ghost of Stephen's mother, reminiscent of the "ghostly" gaslight in "The Dead" which ushers in the spirit of Michael and allows the dead Mrs. Rowan her entrance into the affairs of Gretta and Gabriel. Stephen's assault on the gas-jet is for him a very real assault on the ghost of his mother; the "pwfungg" of the gas a sign of her demise. She has also been reflected in the images of the Nighttown whores, the pseudo-brides of Dublin, corrupt much in the manner of the maternal corpse-bride: "(Stephen's mother, emaciated, rises stark through the floor in leper grey with a wreath of faded orange blossoms and a torn bridal veil, her face worn and noseless, green with grave mould. Her hair is scant and lank. She fixes her bluecircled hollow eyesockets on Stephen and opens her toothless mouth uttering a silent word.)" (p. 564). Unable to subdue her son, this green corpse-bride, with "a green rill of bile" trickling from the side of her mouth, at last stretches a "blackened, withered right arm slowly towards Stephen's breast with outstretched fingers." This final gesture of dominion Stephen sees as

"God's hand: (A green crab with malignant red eyes sticks deep its grinning claws in Stephen's heart.)" (p. 567). God, a shout in the Dublin Street, the red-rimmed horny eyes of Irish peasantry (in *A Portrait*), the Nighttown whores, Stephen's mother, coalesce in the grisly image of a grinning crab. In this image Joyce compresses Stephen's nightmare of history, the personal and racial unconscious. It is after all a *gesture* of dominion, and only a *gesture* of liberation will serve to pry it from his heart. After his firm *Non Serviam*, Stephen: "lifts his ashplant high with both hands" and smashes the chandelier. "Time's livid final flame leaps and, in the following darkness, ruin of all space, shattered glass and toppling masonry" (pp. 567–568). The gas jet has a final word: "Pwfungg!" Presumably, the ghost of Stephen's mother is no more.

As an artist, Stephen has sought throughout *Ulysses* "the form of forms" which would free him from the personal and racial unconscious. This form is the principle of vital, as opposed to mechanical, activity. Because his oppression is so bound up with a repressive, mechanistic use of language, his liberation, that is to say his search for the "form of forms" becomes a quest for an effective *gesture* of liberation which will replace an ineffectual verbal formula. The artfully loquacious Dubliners, and the pedantically articulate Richard Rowan, had coped with their oppression largely by manipulative strategies of language. But in *Ulysses*, Stephen Dedalus realized that he could only deal with the oppressor in his head by a gesture of exorcism, his shattering of the brothel light.

This method and the meaning of his gesture are forecast early in "Circe," where the Nighttown light merges with the "light of love," the female domination of "shrewridden Shakespeare and henpecked Socrates. Even the allwisest stagyrite [Aristotle] was bitted, bridled, and mounted by a light of love" (p. 245). Just before saying this to the ubiquitous Lynch, Stephen had flourished his ashplant, "shivering the lamp image, shattering light over the world," replying to Lynch's "so that," with an explanation of gesture as "a universal language, the gift of tongues rendering visible not the lay sense but the first entelechy, the structural rhythm" (p. 425). Stephen's quest for a "structural rhythm" obliges him to destroy the ghost of his mother, the "light of love," begging him from the grave to repeat a ritual formula of language. She wishes him to accompany his prayer with a gesture of allegiance to her spirit—a submissive kneeling beside her bed. He will do neither, because he will not play a dictated role. His rude gesture of liberation is uniquely his own.

Yet, the true hero of *Ulysses* is Leopold Bloom, the most rounded version in literature of a sadomasochist. He would seem to contradict Joyce's wish to heal his city by giving it a thorough look at itself in the mirror of his art, for in that mirror, the paralytic self-frustration of Dublin is sadomasochistic neurosis. Though one should have expected Bloom to be Joyce's explicit version of health, it is difficult to study *Ulysses* without concluding that Bloom epitomizes the impotence Joyce despised in Dublin. His tendency to restore a lost potency by vicarious contact with that of other men, exhibited in detail in "Sirens," his inclination for erotic torture and submission catalogued in "Circe," his secret plots for intricate revenge before falling asleep in Eccles Street—these would seem to grow out of that same deep instinct for self-betrayal and for secret manipulation of others Joyce meticulously described in his earlier fiction.

But Joyce himself loved Bloom; critics have been almost unanimous in their affection for him; he has become an exemplum of modern heroism in the face of the commonplace attrition of daily life. I think we may account for Bloom if we assume the absolute necessity for Stephen to be purified of neurotic response, as this purgation has been detailed throughout *A Portrait* and *Ulysses*. He had to become the undominated artist to confront his material, the habitual perversity of Dublin, with objective benevolence. If Bloom is Dublin writ in detail, then he is also the perversity of Dublin, just as he avoids a half-hearted indulgence in that perversity by virtue of an Odyssean magnanimity. Stephen must eject maternal imperium just as he must eject political, religious, social imperium, because he is an artist, and an artist cannot allow himself to be dominated by the roles he must discern and describe. If he must be outside and inside the narrative, he cannot at the same time be lured back *under* the surface of Dublin life, into the demonic underworld. Neither can he allow the distortion of his perception by a hostility still operating out of immersion in the demonic unconscious. Like Joyce himself, Stephen must be able to see things as they are, and, seeing them, sympathize in the manner of Flaubert, whose final attitude was one of compassion for what man was called upon to endure. Furthermore, though the shrewd eye of the true artist might perceive with compassion both the indignities and the beauties of daily life, he must not blind himself to the way in which man makes use of these in not altogether benign ways. If Bloom has appeared to critics as a Joycean version of the liberal humanist or baroque Catholic saint he has also appeared as a kind of moral failure.[6] From the perspective of Stephen-Joyce, he may have been both, but it is the aesthetic perception which elevates him into a hero for this age. In short, Bloom is *made* beautiful for our eyes. The making beautiful of much that is ugly is the achievement of a splendid artist. But victory over his material must be that of one who has cast from his eye the beam of contempt.

Few episodes in *Ulysses* demonstrate the generation of beauty from unabashedly sordid material as well as the "Sirens" episode. Here we observe the operation of that same instinct for sadomasochistic manipulation, vicarious erotic experience, psychic and sexual impotence, that same submission to various kinds of imperium present everywhere else in Joyce. But here, Joyce infuses these sordid facts of human behavior with extraordinary feeling.

Absorbed in the forthcoming liaison between Molly and Boylan, Bloom experiences both how he imagines Molly to respond and

[6] These three versions of Bloom can be attributed respectively to Richard Kain, *Fabulous Voyager: James Joyce's "Ulysses"* (New York, 1959); Stanley Sultan, *The Argument of "Ulysses"* (Columbus, 1964); Darcy O'Brien, *The Conscience of James Joyce* (Princeton, 1968).

what he imagines Boylan to achieve. Identifying with Molly he experiences her feeling of having been conquered, as she recalls before sleeping, "he must have come 3 or 4 times with that tremendous big red brute of a thing he has . . . like a Stallion driving it up into you . . . with that determined vicious look in his eye" (p. 727). At the same time Bloom identifies with Boylan whose assignation he not only does nothing to obstruct but has helped arrange by introducing them. In *The Making of "Ulysses"* Frank Budgen perceived the homosexual implications of Bloom's attitude towards his own cuckholding,[7] but I think Joyce emphasized something different. Despite the extent of his identification with Molly during her intercourse with Boylan, the overriding impression in "Sirens" is that Bloom's basic drive is heterosexual. He may identify with Molly at some level, but he shares a deeper identification with Boylan, as though by sharing Boylan's determined sexuality he could feel again the potency diminished since Rudy's death. The basic identification with Boylan is clear from what Bloom does and imagines during "Sirens." Listening to the music and fantasying the lush pleasure in his own bedroom, he acts out manually Boylan's sexual penetration: "Bloom unwound slowly the elastic band of his packet . . . wound the skein round four forkfingers, stretched it, relaxed, and wound it round his troubled double, fourfold, in octave, gyved [shackled] them fast" (p. 269). However surrogate, this manual phallic activity is the outcome of masculine identification, the elastic band a substitute for Molly's vagina. Furthermore, Bloom participates vicariously in the triumphant rise of the tenor's voice at the same time he imagines Boylan's triumphant erection. With astounding skill Joyce conveys the sense of Bloom's delightful acquiescence in the triumph of both voice and phallus:

[7] "Linked to the fatalism of the Orient and organically connected with his Jewish and personal masochism is the homosexual wish to share his wife with other men." Frank Budgen, *James Joyce and the Making of "Ulysses"* (London, 1937), p. 149.

Tenderness it welled: slow, swelling. Full it throbbed. That's the chat. Ha, give! Take! Throb, a throb, a pulsing proud erect. Words? Music? No: it's what's behind.

Bloom looped, unlooped, noded, disnoded.

Bloom. Flood of warm jimjam lickitup secretness flowed to flow in music out, in desire, dark to lick flow, invading. Tipping her tepping her tapping her topping her. Tup. Pores to dilate dilating. Tup. The joy the feel the warm the. Tup. To pour o'er sluices pouring gushes. Flood, gush, flow, joygush, tupthrop. Now! Language of love (p. 270).

Merging this description of coition with music, Joyce conveys Bloom's struggle to feel again his lost potency. Because he has been able in fantasy to precipitate a beatific orgasm, he can now imagine a successful liaison with his epistolary Martha, once again fantasying in harmony with music:

Quitting all languor Lionel cried in grief, in cry of passion dominant to love to return with deepening yet with rising chords of harmony. In cry of lionel loneliness that she should know, must Martha feel. For only her he waited. Where? Here there try there here all try where. Somewhere.

—*Co-me, thou lost one!*

Co-me thou dear one!

Alone. One love. One hope. One comfort me. Martha, chestnote, return.

—*Come!*

It soared, a bird, it held its flight, a swift pure cry, soar silver orb it leaped serene, speeding, sustained, to come, don't spin it out too long long he breath long life, soaring high, high resplendent, aflame, crowned, high in the effulgence symbolistic, high, of the ethereal bosom, high, of the high vast irradiation everywhere all soaring around about the all, the endless*nessnessness* . . .

—*To me!*

Siopold!

Consumed.

Come. Well sung. All clapped. She ought to.

Come. To, me, to him, to her, You too, me, us. (p. 271)

Granted Joyce's prodigious achievement, in Leopold and Molly Bloom a spectacular aesthetic transcendence of the Dublin perversities which drove Joyce at one time to wish for venom in his inkwell, one must finally conclude that beauty was not enough. To review briefly the process Joyce described is quickly to perceive the final inconclusiveness of that process. Paralyzed by a demonic mythology, the Dubliners required the redemptive intervention of a culture hero. *A Portrait* describes the embryology of this hero, the isolated artist, identified with Icarus-Daedalus, poised on the eastern shore of that mad Ireland which hurt Joyce into poetry as effectively as it hurt the Yeats of Auden's splendid elegy. Ireland, his in part self-created labyrinth, forces him to plot the forgery of a new conscience for his race. *Ulysses* reveals this culture-hero fallen on bad times, aware of the inadequacy of isolated aesthetic perception to save either himself or his race. At this point, the quest begins for a somatic father and for a mother who will "make him feel all over him" (p. 761) as Molly imagines, instead of feeding him only brain food (p. 566), as his mother had. Both Leopold and Molly Bloom revel in the life of touch and together appear designed to restore to Stephen the body he had lost in infancy. Insofar as the book describes the contour of Stephen's recapture of that rich capacity for sensation repressed by the flesh hatred of Dublin, it may be said to move from cerebrum to touch. Here is where the mode changes from the chiefly ironic possibly cynical perceptions of *Dubliners* to the mythological perceptions of *A Portrait* and the "Romantic" perceptions of *Ulysses*. Without something corresponding to supernatural intervention, neither the culture hero nor his people can transcend the tightly woven nets of Ireland, for these nets are both internal and external, psychological sadomasochism, religious and political imperialism, economic servitude, within a context of deplorable self-deception. Supernatural intervention is the means by which the typical romantic hero overcomes the conditions of environment,[8] which

[8] Northrop Frye, *Anatomy of Criticism* (Princeton, 1957), p. 33.

Joyce summed up in the notion of history as nightmare. Thus, in defining Stephen as a romantic hero, as a Telemachus-Hamlet, Joyce met head on the problem of discovering an adequate mode of awakening from the nightmare of history, much as though if Hamlet could have awakened from his dream his quest would have succeeded. Stephen's personal awakening from the nightmare will then presumably allow him to go about awakening his compatriots. He confronts the nightmare of repressed maternal imperium and exorcises it not so much by magic as by an act of will. At this point godlike Joyce himself enters the picture, which is to say that his is the "supernatural" intervention. He must provide the power by which his Bloom, the quintessence of a Dubliner, can transcend the slavery of Dublin, "saved" by the transubstantiation of daily experience in an aesthetic mass. In Bloom, Joyce suffers to make of the Dubliners what the "fallen" nature of Ireland will not allow, heroes who transcend the limitations of everyday life by immersing themselves in it. In this acceptance they are elevated to the ancient condition of romantic heroes, Odysseus, of course, chief among them.

The artist can perhaps only accomplish his redemption by a kind of aesthetic forgery, hammered out in the smithy of his own soul. Stephen and Bloom do not unite as father and son. Stephen will probably not return for Molly to "make him feel all over him." Bloom will remain impotent, as his final osculation of Molly's rump implies. A transformation of their condition occurs only in the imaginations of Joyce, of the reader, of Bloom and Molly themselves. Though Stephen may slay the demons of Ireland and perhaps, as in "Proteus," redeem his own perception, and manage a humanely comic view, he remains isolated from the human community at the end of *Ulysses*. Similar truths may be elicited concerning Bloom. After all he is Joyce's great hero in the end, and when all is said and done he remains a sadomasochist, devoted much like his predecessors to neurotic vicarious experience. As a therapeutic document, *Ulysses* was only partially successful.

BIBLIOGRAPHY

Works by James Joyce

Joyce, James. *The Critical Writings of James Joyce*. Edited by Richard Ellmann and Ellsworth Mason. New York: Viking, 1967.
———. *Dubliners*. New York: Viking, 1967.
———. *Exiles*. New York: Viking, 1965.
———. *Finnegans Wake*. New York: Viking, 1958.
———. *Giacomo Joyce*. Edited with an introduction by Richard Ellmann. New York: Viking, 1968.
———. *Letters*. Volume 1 edited by Stuart Gilbert, volumes 2 and 3 edited by Richard Ellmann. New York: Viking, 1966.
———. *The Portable James Joyce*. Edited by Harry Levin. New York: Viking, 1959.
———. *A Portrait of the Artist as a Young Man*. New York: Viking, 1966.
———. *Ulysses*. New York: Random House, 1946.

Other Works Cited

Adams, Robert. "Light on Joyce's *Exiles?* A New MS, a Curious Analogue, and Some Speculations." *Studies in Bibliography* 17 (1964): 83–105.
Albert, Leonard. "James Joyce and the New Psychology." Ph.D. dissertation. New York: Columbia University, 1957.
Balfe, M. W. *The Bohemian Girl*. Libretto by A. Bunn. New York: W. Corbyn, 185[?].
Blotner, Joseph L. " 'Ivy Day in the Committee Room': Death Without Resurrection." *Perspective* 9 (Summer, 1957): 210–217.
Brooks, Cleanth, and Robert Penn Warren, eds. *Understanding Fiction*. New York: Appleton, 1959.
Browne, Ray; William Roscelli; and Richard Loftus, eds. *The Celtic Cross*. West Lafayette: Purdue University Press, 1964.

Budgen, Frank. *James Joyce and the Making of "Ulysses."* London: Grayson and Grayson, 1937.

Burke, Kenneth. "Three Definitions: The Joyce Portrait." *Kenyon Review* 13 (Spring, 1951): 181–192.

Campbell, Joseph. *The Masks of God: Primitive Mythology.* New York: Viking, 1965.

Carpenter, Richard, and Daniel Leary. "The Witch Maria." *James Joyce Review* 3, nos. 1 and 2 (February, 1959): 3–7.

Catholic Encyclopedia. Edited by Charles G. Herbermann *et al.* 15 volumes. New York: Appleton, 1907–1912.

Colum, Mary, and Padraic Colum. *Our Friend James Joyce.* New York: Doubleday, 1958.

Daiches, David. *The Novel and the Modern World.* Chicago: University of Chicago Press, 1960.

de Sade, Donatien-Alphonse-Francois [the Marquis de Sade]. *The Complete Justine, Philosophy in the Bedroom, and Other Writings.* Compiled and translated by Richard Seaver and Austryn Wainhouse. New York: Grove Press, 1966.

―――. *The 120 Days of Sodom and Other Writings.* Compiled and translated by Austryn Wainhouse and Richard Seaver. New York: Grove Press, 1967.

Donoghue, Denis. "Joyce and the Finite Order." *Sewanee Review* 68 (Spring, 1960): 256–273.

Edel, Leon. "Notes on the Use of Psychological Tools in Literary Scholarship." *Newsletter of the Conference on Literature and Psychology of the Modern Language Association* 1 (September, 1951): 1–3.

Ellison, Ralph. *Invisible Man.* New York: New American Library, 1964.

Ellmann, Richard. *James Joyce.* New York: Oxford University Press, 1959.

Fergusson, Francis. *The Idea of a Theatre.* New York: Doubleday, 1953.

Ferrero, Guglielmo. *L'Europa giovane.* Milan: Treves, 1897.

Freud, Sigmund. *Collected Papers.* Volume 4. Translated under the supervision of Joan Riviere. New York: Basic Books, 1959.

Friedrich, Gerhard. "Bret Harte as a Source for James Joyce's 'The Dead.'" *Philological Quarterly* 33 (October, 1954): 442–444.

―――. "The Gnomonic Clue to James Joyce's *Dubliners.*" *MLN* 72 (June, 1957): 421–424.

Frye, Northrop. *Anatomy of Criticism.* Princeton, N.J.: Princeton University Press, 1957.

Ghiselin, Brewster. "The Unity of Joyce's *Dubliners*." *Accent* 16 (Spring, 1956): 75–88; (Summer, 1956): 196–213.

Gilbert, Stuart. *James Joyce's "Ulysses."* New York: Random House, 1952.

Giraud, Raymond, ed. *Flaubert: A Collection of Critical Essays.* Englewood Cliffs, N.J.: Prentice-Hall, 1964.

Givens, Sean, ed. *James Joyce: Two Decades of Criticism.* New York: Vanguard, 1948.

Guerard, Albert. *Thomas Hardy: The Novels and Stories.* Cambridge: Harvard University Press, 1949.

Hayman, David. "Forms of Folly in Joyce: A Study of Clowning in *Ulysses.*" *ELH* 34, no. 2 (June, 1967): 260–283.

Holland, Norman. *The Dynamics of Literary Response.* New York: Oxford University Press, 1968.

Hudson, Richard B. "Joyce's 'Clay.' " *The Explicator* 6 (March, 1948): Item 30.

Huizinga, Johan. *Homo Ludens: A Study of the Play-Element in Culture.* Boston: Beacon Press, 1966.

Huysmans, J. K. *Against Nature.* Translated by Robert Baldick. Baltimore: Penguin, 1959.

Ibsen, Henrik. *Last Plays of Henrik Ibsen.* Translated by Arvid Paulson. New York: Bantam, 1962.

Jones, Ernest. *Papers on Psychoanalysis.* Boston: Beacon Press, 1961.

Josephson, Matthew. *Zola and His Time.* New York: Book League of America, 1928.

Joyce, Stanislaus. *My Brother's Keeper: James Joyce's Early Years.* New York: Viking, 1958.

Kain, Richard. *Fabulous Voyager: James Joyce's "Ulysses."* New York: Viking, 1959.

Kaye, Julian B. "The Wings of Daedalus: Two Stories in *Dubliners.*" *Modern Fiction Studies* 4 (Spring, 1958): 31–41.

Kenner, Hugh. "Joyce's *Exiles.*" *Hudson Review* 5 (Autumn, 1952): 389–403.

Kosinski, Jerzy. *The Painted Bird.* New York: Pocket Books, 1967.

Lawrence, D. H. *D. H. Lawrence: Four Short Novels.* New York: Viking, 1965.

———. *Psychoanalysis and the Unconscious* and *Fantasia of the Unconscious.* New York: Viking, 1962.

Lesser, Simon O. *Fiction and the Unconscious.* New York: Random House, 1962.

Levin, Harry. *James Joyce: A Critical Introduction.* Norfolk: New Directions, 1941.

Levin, Richard, and Charles Shattuck. "First Flight to Ithaca: A New Reading of Joyce's *Dubliners.*" *Accent* 4 (Winter, 1944): 75–99.

McCarthy, Mary. Foreward to *Madame Bovary.* New York: New American Library, 1964.

Magalaner, Marvin. "James Joyce's *Dubliners.*" Ph.D. dissertation. New York: Columbia University, 1951.

————. *A James Joyce Miscellany, third series.* Carbondale: Southern Illinois University Press, 1962.

———— and Richard M. Kain. *Joyce: The Man, the Work, the Reputation.* New York: Collier Books, 1962.

————. "Joyce, Nietzsche, and Hauptmann in James Joyce's 'A Painful Case,' " *PMLA* 68 (March, 1953): 95–102.

————. "The Other Side of James Joyce." *Arizona Quarterly* 9 (Spring, 1953): 5–16.

————. *Time of Apprenticeship: The Fiction of Young James Joyce.* New York: Abelard-Schuman, 1959.

Manheim, Leonard and Eleanor Manheim, eds. *Hidden Patterns: Studies in Psychoanalytic Literary Criticism.* New York: Macmillan, 1966.

Mann, Thomas. "The Making of *The Magic Mountain.*" In *The Magic Mountain.* Translated by H. T. Lowe-Porter. New York: Random House, 1953.

Mathews, F. X. "Punchestime: A New Look at 'Clay.' " *James Joyce Quarterly* 4, no. 2 (Winter, 1967): 102–106.

Nietzsche, Friedrich. *The Genealogy of Morals.* Translated by Francis Golffing. New York: Doubleday, 1956.

————. *Thus Spoke Zarathustra.* Edited by Manuel Komroff. New York: Tudor, 1934.

Noon, William T. "Joyce's 'Clay': An Interpretation." *College English* 17 (November, 1955): 93–95.

O'Brien, Darcy. *The Conscience of James Joyce.* Princeton: Princeton University Press, 1968.

Phillips, William, ed. *Art and Psychoanalysis.* New York: World, 1967.

Pound, Ezra. *Pound/Joyce: The Letters of Ezra Pound to James Joyce, with Pound's Essays on Joyce.* Edited with commentary by Forrest Read. New York: New Directions, 1967.

Praz, Mario. *The Romantic Agony.* Translated by Angus Davidson. New York: Oxford, 1951.

Réage, Pauline. *The Story of O.* Translated by Sabine d'Estrée. New York: Grove Press, 1967.

Redwine, James D., Jr. "Beyond Psychology: The Moral Basis of Jonson's Theory of Humour Characterization." *ELH* 28, no. 3 (September, 1961): 316–334.

Ruitenbeek, Hendrik M., ed. *Psychoanalysis and Literature.* New York: Dutton, 1964.

Sacher-Masoch, Leopold von. *Venus in Furs.* New York: Belmont Books, 1965.

Scholes, Robert. *The Cornell Joyce Collection.* Ithaca: Cornell University Press, 1961.

————. "Further Observations on the Text of *Dubliners.*" *Studies in Bibliography* 17 (1964): 107–122.

————. "Grant Richards to James Joyce." *Studies in Bibliography* 16 (1963): 139–160.

————. "Some Observations on the Text of *Dubliners*: 'The Dead.'" *Studies in Bibliography* 15 (1962): 191–205.

Schorer, Mark, ed. *The Story: A Critical Anthology.* New York: Prentice-Hall, 1950.

Schwartz, Charleen M. *Neurotic Anxiety.* New York: Sheed and Ward, 1954.

Short, Clarice. "Joyce's 'A Little Cloud.'" *MLN* 72 (April, 1957): 275–278.

Solotaroff, Theodore, ed. *New American Review 7.* New York: New American Library, 1969.

Starkie, Enid. *Flaubert: The Making of the Master.* New York: Atheneum, 1967.

Steinberg, Edwin R. "A Book with a Molly in It." *James Joyce Review* 2, nos. 1 and 2 (June, 1958): 55–62.

Stein, William B. "'Counterparts': A Swine Song." *James Joyce Quarterly* 1, no. 2 (Winter, 1964): 30–32.

Stekel, Wilhelm. *Sadism and Masochism: The Psychology of Hatred and Cruelty.* Translated by Louise Brink, 2 volumes. New York: Grove Press, 1963.

Stone, Harry. "'Araby' and the Writings of James Joyce." *The Antioch Review* 25 (Fall, 1965): 375–410.

Sultan, Stanley. *The Argument of "Ulysses."* Columbus: Ohio State University Press, 1964.

Thorpe, James, ed. *Relations of Literary Study: Essays on Interdisci-*

plinary Contributions. New York: Modern Language Association of America, 1967.

Tindall, W. Y. *James Joyce: His Way of Interpreting the Modern World.* New York: Scribner's, 1950.

―――. *A Reader's Guide to James Joyce.* New York: Noonday, 1959.

Tolstoy, Leo. *The Death of Ivan Ilych and Other Stories.* Translated by Aylmer Maude. New York: New American Library, 1960.

Walzl, Florence L. "Gabriel and Michael: The Conclusion of 'The Dead.' " *James Joyce Quarterly* 4, no. 1 (Fall, 1966): 17–31.

INDEX

The Abbot, 51
Adams, Robert, 127, 128n, 132, 136
"After the Race," 28, 83–88, 92
Against Nature, 9–12
Alleyne, Mr. (in "Counterparts"), 104–107
Alphy (in "Clay"), 70
Anatomy of Criticism, 49, 157–158
Anna Karenina, 75
"Araby," 27, 28, 35, 49–56, 60, 67, 71, 85, 86
Arendt, Hannah, 34
Aristotle, 6, 25
Arnall, Father (in *A Portrait of the Artist*), 162–163

Balfe, M. W., 62–63, 67, 71, 72
"The Ballad of Persse O'Reilly," 105n
Beckett, Samuel, 149
Bertha (in *Exiles*), 138, 139–140, 141, 142, 143, 144–145, 151, 155, 157
Bismarck, Otto, 97
Bloom, Leopold (in *Ulysses*), 3, 11, 12, 14, 24, 93, 94, 100, 103, 114, 130, 157, 160, 168–173
Bloom, Molly (in *Ulysses*), 12, 24, 93, 98, 100, 103–104, 143, 169, 170, 172, 173
Blotner, Joseph L., 109n
"The Boarding House," 30, 31–32, 46, 54, 121n
The Bohemian Girl, 62–63, 72, 87
Boylan, Blazes (in *Ulysses*), 93, 169, 170
Brooks, Cleanth, 50n–51n
Browning, Robert, 117
Budgen, Frank, 170
Burke, Kenneth, 115n
Burroughs, William, 11

Butler, Father (in "An Encounter"), 45
Byron, George Gordon, 101, 104

Campbell, Joseph, 26n
Carmen, 135
Cervantes, 7
Chaucer, 51
Chekov, Anton, 76
Christ: and Parnell, 109n
"Circe," 166, 167, 168
"Clay," 28, 29, 57, 58, 67–73, 76, 88, 100n
Colgan (in "Ivy Day in the Committee Room"), 112, 113
Conroy, Gabriel (in "The Dead"), 22n, 26, 27, 35, 50, 93, 116–125, 129, 131, 134, 139, 141, 142, 164, 166
Conroy, Gretta (in "The Dead"), 50, 56, 116, 119, 120, 122, 123, 124, 142, 144, 146, 166
Corley (in "Two Gallants"), 88–97, 101
"Counterparts," 29, 83, 104–107
Cranly (in *A Portrait of the Artist*), 93
Crofton, Mr. (in "Ivy Day in the Committee Room"), 115
Curran, Constantine, 22n, 31

Daiches, David, 115n–116n
Dante Alighieri, 163
"The Dead," 13, 14, 22, 26–30, 35, 50, 52, 56, 73, 76, 110, 115–126, 130, 131, 134, 139, 142, 146, 156, 164, 165, 166
"The Death of Ivan Ilych," 8–9
Dedalus, Stephen (in *A Portrait of the Artist*), 3, 20, 26, 31, 48n, 55, 93, 116,

124, 125–126, 127, 134, 136, 140, 159–164, 165–168, 169
de Sade, Marquis, 11–12, 29, 33, 34, 48, 128, 142, 143, 154
The Devout Communicant, 51
Dillon, Leo (in "An Encounter"), 45
A Doll's House, 130
Donoghue, Denis, 55n
Don Quixote, 7
Doran, Bob (in "A Boarding House"), 32, 32n, 116
Dostoevsky, Feodor, 8
Doyle, Jimmy (in "After the Race"), 28, 83–88, 92, 116
Duffy, James (in "A Painful Case"), 9, 26, 35, 50, 52, 56, 58, 73–82, 116, 125, 134

Earwicker, H. C. (in *Finnegans Wake*), 74, 130
Edel, Leon, 4
Edward, King, 112, 115
Eichmann, 34
Eliza (in "The Sisters"), 40, 42
Ellison, Ralph, 159
Ellmann, Richard, 5–6, 13, 22n, 147, 152
Emma (in *A Portrait of the Artist*), 93, 124
"An Encounter," 26, 35, 41, 45–49, 59, 60, 64, 69, 74, 77, 85, 88, 114, 142
Endgame, 149
An Enemy of the People, 148n
L'Europa giovane, 96–98
"Eveline," 26, 57, 58–67, 69, 70, 71, 88, 134, 160, 164
Eveline (in "Eveline"), 26–27, 56, 58, 61–65, 87, 88, 116, 134, 144
Exiles, 3, 12, 15n, 27, 29, 30, 47, 93, 127–158, 161, 164, 166

Farrington (in "Counterparts"), 29, 83, 104–107, 116
Fergusson, Francis, 132
Ferrero, Guglielmo, 96–98
Fiction and the Unconscious, 6–7
Finnegans Wake, 20, 31, 37, 74, 76, 105n, 127, 130

Flaubert, Gustave, 7–8, 9, 14, 169
Flynn, Father (in "The Sisters"), 9, 27, 114, 118
"The Fox," 59–60
Frank (in "Eveline"), 58, 59, 60, 61, 62, 64, 65, 69, 87
Freud, Sigmund, 5, 20, 165
Friedrich, Gerhard, 41n, 120n
Frye, Northrop, 49, 151–152, 153, 154, 156, 157–158
Furey, Michael (in "The Dead"), 93, 116, 119–120, 121, 122, 123, 142, 166

Gabriel Conroy, 120n
Gallagher, Dr. Charleen Schwartz, vii
Gallaher, Ignatius (in "A Little Cloud"), 69, 99–103
The Genealogy of Morals, 81–82
Ghiselin, Brewster, 86, 87, 121n
Giacomo Joyce, 146–148
Gilbert, Stuart, 98
Gogol, Nikolay, 8
"Grace," 28, 30, 116
Griffin, William J., 3
Guerard, Albert, 30

Hamlet, 173
Hand, Robert (in *Exiles*), 128–129, 133, 134, 136, 137, 141, 144, 150, 152, 155, 157
Hardy, Thomas, 30
Harte, Bret, 120n
Hayman, David, 150–151, 156
Hedda Gabbler, 148, 148n
Henchy, Mr. (in "Ivy Day in the Committee Room"), 109n, 113, 114, 115
Henchy, Patrick, 62
Holland, Norman, 5, 5n
Holohan, Hoppy (in "A Mother"), 116
Hudson, Richard, 73n
Humpty Dumpty, 105, 105n
Huysmans, J. K., 9–12
Hynes, Mr. (in "Ivy Day in the Committee Room"), 109, 109n, 111–114

Ibsen, Henrik, 27, 30, 110, 124–125, 148, 148n, 153

Idea of a Theatre, 132
Invisible Man, 159
Ivors, Miss (in "The Dead"), 117, 119, 123
"Ivy Day in the Committee Room," 28, 30, 73, 109–115, 116

Joe (in "Clay"), 70, 73
Jones, Ernest, 23–24
Jonson, Ben, 152–153
Joyce, Lucia, 6
Joyce, Nora, 5, 13, 15–18, 24, 54, 90n, 94n, 99
Joyce, Stanislaus, 5, 15, 15n, 21, 31, 41, 46, 69, 74, 75, 82n, 92, 99, 106, 110, 148
Julia (in "The Dead"), 118
Jung, Dr. C. G., 6
Justice, Beatrice (in *Exiles*), 128–129, 133, 134, 135, 143, 144–145

Kaye, Julian B., 44n, 99n
Kearney, Mrs. (in "A Mother"), 107
Kenner, Hugh, 127, 131, 133, 134, 137n
Keon, Father (in "Ivy Day in the Committee Room"), 113, 114

Lawrence, D. H., 57, 59–60, 89
Lenehan (in "Two Gallants"), 83, 88–97, 99, 101, 116, 140, 141
Lesser, Simon O., 5, 6–7
Levin, Harry, 98, 127
Levin, Richard, 74n
Lily (in "The Dead"), 116–117
Little Chandler (in "A Little Cloud"), 35, 69, 83, 99–103, 105, 116, 121n
"A Little Cloud," 35, 69, 83, 99–104, 105, 121n
Love's Labor's Lost, 154
Lynch (in *Ulysses*), 167
Lyons, Emily (in notes to *Exiles*), 145, 146

McCarthy, Mary, 14
MacDowell, Gerty (in *Ulysses*), 12, 143
Macool, Finn (in *Finnegans Wake*), 74
Madame Bovary, 7–8

Magalaner, Marvin, 32n, 37n, 46, 47, 65, 68, 70, 73n, 80n, 100n
The Magic Mountain, 18–19
Mahoney (in "An Encounter"), 48–49
The Making of Ulysses, 170
Malins, Freddy (in "The Dead"), 121
Malins, Mrs. (in "The Dead"), 119
Mangan (in "Araby"), 53, 54
Mann, Thomas, 18–19, 20
Margaret Mary Alacoque, St., 65–66
Maria (in "Clay"), 28, 29, 58, 67–73, 76, 88, 100n, 116, 144
Mary Jane (in "The Dead"), 118, 123
The Memoirs of Vidocq, 51
Millet, Kate, 12n
Morkan, Patrick (in "The Dead"), 75, 156
Morse, J. Mitchell, 98
"A Mother," 30, 46, 107
My Brother's Keeper, 74, 82n, 99

Naked Lunch, 11
Nannie (in "The Sisters"), 42
Neurotic Anxiety, vii
Nietzsche, Friedrich, 81–82, 148
Noon, William T., 73n
The Novel and the Modern World, 115n

O'Brien, Darcy, 129n
O'Connor (in "Ivy Day in the Committee Room"), 109n, 111, 112, 114
Oedipus Rex, 132
Old Cotter (in "The Sisters"), 36, 37, 39
Old Jack (in "Ivy Day in the Committee Room"), 114
The 120 Days of Sodom, 154n
"On the Death of a Young Lady," 101
The Overcoat, 8

"A Painful Case," 9, 25n, 26, 28, 50, 52, 57, 58, 73–82, 125, 134
The Painted Bird, 33
Parnell, Charles Stewart, 28, 109, 109n, 110–111, 112, 113, 115
Phillips, William, 4
Philosophy in the Bedroom, 11, 143

The Poetics, 6
Polly (in "A Boarding House"), 53
A Portrait of the Artist as a Young Man, 3, 15, 15n, 18, 20, 26, 37, 48n, 55, 93, 116, 124, 125, 127, 136, 140, 147, 159, 160–165, 168, 172
Pound, Ezra, 127, 130, 132, 148–150, 151, 154
Praz, Mario, 11
Psychoanalysis and the Unconscious, 57
Pyrrhus, 31

Rank, Otto, 20n
A Rebours, 11
Richards, Grant, 32, 44, 95, 96
The Romantic Agony, 11
Rousset, Jean, 7
Rowan, Mrs. (in *Exiles*), 136, 139, 166
Rowan, Richard (in *Exiles*), 93, 127, 128–146, 149, 151, 153, 155–156, 157, 158, 161, 167

Sacher-Masoch, Leopold von, 11, 29, 33, 34, 48, 128, 143, 154
Sacred Heart, 65n
Schorer, Mark, 100n
Scott, Sir Walter, 51
Shattuck, Charles, 74n
Shaw, Bernard, 148
Short, Clarice, 101n
Sinico, Emily (in "A Painful Case"), 77–78, 79, 81, 144
"Sirens," 168
"The Sisters," 9, 22, 27, 29, 35–45, 47, 49, 51, 58, 60, 64, 65, 88, 114, 118
Smith, Roland, 62

Starkie, Enid, 7, 14
Steinberg, Edwin R., 98
Stein, William B., 107n
Stekel, Wilhelm, 22, 88–89, 91, 93, 106, 138, 156, 157
Stendhal, 9
Stephen Hero, 15n, 140
Stone, Harry, 54n
The Story of O, 33
Swift, Jonathan, 137

Thrane, James R., 162n
Thus Spoke Zarathustra, 82n
Tierney, Mr. (in "Ivy Day in the Committee Room"), 110, 112, 113
Tindall, W. Y., 32, 46, 62, 98
Tolstoy, Leo, 8–9, 75, 76
Trilling, Lionel, 5
"Two Gallants," 83, 88–99, 102, 103, 140

Ulysses, 3, 12, 14, 15, 18, 20, 28, 29, 31, 37, 46, 74, 89, 93, 98, 103–104, 111, 114, 116, 126, 127, 130, 134, 135, 144, 147, 157, 159, 160, 164, 165–173

Venus in Furs, 33, 143, 157
Villona (in "After the Race"), 84, 86

Walzl, Florence L., 119n
Wasserstrom, William, 20n, 165n
When We Dead Awaken, 110, 124–125, 148n
Wilde, Oscar, 148

Zola, Emile, 32, 32n

A Note on the Author

Edward Brandabur is associate professor of English at the University of Illinois at Urbana-Champaign. He has taught modern literature at Illinois since receiving his doctorate in 1961 from the University of Cincinnati, where he was a Taft Teaching Fellow. He has published essays on Joyce, Lawrence, and T. S. Eliot and currently is at work on a book-length study of the graphic tradition in modern literature. He lives in Champaign with his wife and seven children.

UNIVERSITY OF ILLINOIS PRESS